A BASIC BOOK OF
AQUARIUMS
LOOK-AND-LEARN

by
DR. HERBERT R. AXELROD

KD-017

Photographs: Dr. Herbert R. Axelrod, K. L. Chew, D. Conkel, J. Elias, S. Franke, Gan Fish Farm, R. Goldstein, H. Grier, B. Kahl, E. Kennedy, D. Kobayashi, A. Kochetov, H. Linke, H. Mayland, A. Norman, J Palicka, R. Pethiyagoda, MP & C. Piednoir, H.-J. Richter, A. Roth, S. Sane, W. Sommer, M. Smith, E. Taylor, K. Tanaka, J. Vierke, S. Yoshino, R. Zukal.

Distributed in the UNITED STATES to the Pet Trade by T.F.H. Publications, Inc., One T.F.H. Plaza, Neptune City, NJ 07753; distributed in the UNITED STATES to the Bookstore and Library Trade by National Book Network, Inc. 4720 Boston Way, Lanham MD 20706; in CANADA to the Pet Trade by H & L Pet Supplies Inc., 27 Kingston Crescent, Kitchener, Ontario N2B 2T6; Rolf C. Hagen Ltd., 3225 Sartelon Street, Montreal 382 Quebec; in CANADA to the Book Trade by Macmillan of Canada (A Division of Canada Publishing Corporation), 164 Commander Boulevard, Agincourt, Ontario M1S 3C7; in the United Kingdom by T.F.H. Publications, PO Eox 15, Waterlooville PO7 6BQ; in AUSTRALIA AND THE SOUTH PACIFIC by T.F.H. (Australia), Pty. Ltd., Box 149, Brookvale 2100 N.S.W., Australia; in NEW ZEALAND by Brooklands Aquarium Ltd. 5 McGiven Drive, New Plymouth, RD1 New Zealand; in Japan by T.F.H. Publications, Japan—Jiro Tsuda, 10-12-3 Ohjidai, Sakura, Chiba 285, Japan; in SOUTH AFRICA by Multipet Pty. Ltd., P.O. Box 35347, Northway, 4065, South Africa. Published by T.F.H. Publications, Inc.

Manufactured in the United States of America by T.F.H. Publications, Inc.

WHY AN AQUARIUM?

Having had aquaria all my life and having worked in the field as editor and publisher of *Tropical Fish Hobbyist Magazine* for over 42 years, I have found the following reasons that people keep aquaria in their homes.

1. Your children get the idea at school and come home with a live goldfish.

2. Your friends or neighbors have an aquarium and encourage you to start by giving you a small, unused aquarium, some fish and lots of advice.

3. You live in an apartment, and want a pet, but birds, dogs and cats are forbidden...so you settle for an aquarium.

4. Your doctor told you to relax and watch something besides television.

5. You want to make pocket money by breeding fishes.

6. You work for a doctor or lawyer who has an aquarium in the waiting room.

7. You read a book or saw beautiful color photographs and became interested in aquariums.

8. You need a night light, so you got a small aquarium on which you leave the light burning all night.

For whatever reason, the fact that you are reading this book indicates that you have an interest in the

Keeping an aquarium is a family affair. Gary shows his and a neighbor's kids how to transfer a fish from an isolation bowl to the main aquarium.

English-speaking world's third largest hobby (after photography and stamp collecting).

It is the purpose of this book to show you the fishes and plants necessary to make a beautiful aquarium, and to tell you how to go about it in a very organized manner.

Aquarium keeping is a FAMILY HOBBY. Get your kids and your spouse interested. Breeding fishes is easy and a necessity for continued interest for children...and a wonderful way to learn the mysteries of the origin of life.

THE AQUARIUM

Starting an aquarium is simple. Go to your local pet shop and buy the largest aquarium you can afford, providing you have the space. The larger the tank the better because cleanliness, removal of pollution from chemicals, temperature maintenance and planting possibilities are easier with a large tank. Only buy from a knowledgeable dealer as you will probably rely upon the dealer for further advice on fishes, equipment and problems of health.

If you want large fishes, you need a large tank. This tank is 100 gallons and contains a large albino Oscar, *Astronotus*, and an Arowana, *Osteoglossum bicirrhosum*. ◗

◆ Discuss with a knowledgeable dealer the costs of the largest tank possible. Remember your tank needs a cover (hood), heater, filter, plants and fishes, as well as a stand upon which to place it.

This goldfish bowl is NOT satisfactory for more than one small goldfish or a large male Siamese Fighting Fish. ◗

▲ A small flat goldfish bowl is preferred to a long, tall one because it gets more oxygen.

Your selection of an aquarium stand depends upon the furniture in your home and the cost. The ideal is a closed cabinet in which paraphernalia can be stored out of sight. ➡

Make sure that the aquarium fits perfectly on the aquarium stand. This should be done BEFORE you buy the tank and stand.

One manufacturer makes a plexiglas tank with a fitted canopy and stand which is beautiful but very expensive. ◗

GETTING STARTED

◀ You should be able to get everything required to start your aquarium at your local aquarium pet store. These are Hagen products shown here.

Plastic aquariums are a necessity as isolation tanks for new arrivals or as a maternity ward. ▶

▲ Complete plastic aquariums, with fitted hoods, are available. This one is a *Hagen Living World TropiQuarium.*

Hagen makes a complete aquarium starter kit which contains almost everything you need to get started. Just add water, plants, fishes and a proper stand or table. ▶

Tanks should be longer than they are tall to ensure a proper exchange of oxygen and carbon dioxide at the water's surface. ▶

If you already have a tank, your dealer can offer a Hagen starter kit which has most of the necessities. These kits are usually cheaper than buying the items separately.

◀ These are *quarter* tanks, each one being a 90° angle. The tanks are separate but they look like one since the side glasses are invisible.

◀ Make sure that the equipment you buy is made by a substantial manufacturer. Some dealers sell a mix of cheap, imported items which are not guaranteed by the DEALER. Read a *TROPICAL FISH HOBBYIST MAGAZINE* to learn the names and addresses of substantial manufacturers.

Your dealer has CYCLE, a necessity for starting an aquarium. It has the bacteria necessary to start organic water conditioning. ▶

GETTING STARTED

◆ Every aquarium must have a hood or canopy on top. This keeps the tank clean, houses the light, prevents evaporation and prevents the fish from jumping out.

◄ The hood or canopy should fit the tank perfectly and should be purchased at the same time you buy your tank.

◄ Do NOT use bottom gravel straight from the bag; wash it thoroughly first and put it in slowly.

◄ If you cannot afford a hood, get a hinged glass top upon which you can add a light.

◄ Once the gravel is in place, pat it to shape it so it slopes from back to front.

➤ Most pet shops have a full assortment of artificial aquarium plants.

◄ You can get colored gravel, plastic plants and artificial ornaments from your local pet shop. Be sure they are made for the aquarium.

With only a few inches of water in the tank, the plants and other decorations can be positioned. Starting with little water is safer since the tank might leak and handling a leaky full tank is difficult. ➤

Don't buy rocks, caves, plants, colored gravel, etc. without a firm plan. ◆

◄ Plastic plants are a necessity in most tanks, even if you have living plants. Your pet shop should have a wide selection of plastic plants. Vibrascaper by Living World is one of the best.

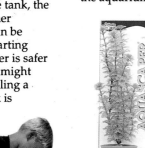

GETTING STARTED

◀ A spawning trap for live-bearers should contain a very bushy plant so the babies can find a place to hide from their cannibalistic mother.

◆ Hagen Algae Magnets allow you to clean your aquarium glass without getting your hands wet.

You can clean the glass by hand with an algae cleaner wand, but the algae magnet is easier. ▶

The Hagen Aquarium Gravel Cleaner allows you to siphon the dirt from the aquarium floor. ▶

The Hagen Multi-Vac is battery powered so you don't need a siphon to clean the gravel. ▶

◀ When first setting up a tank the water must be conditioned by removing chloramine and chlorine, and starting microscopic life. Hagen makes FIN CARE for just this purpose.

◀ Hagen makes a siphon starter that saves the unpleasant sucking experience with which most siphons are started.

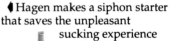

◀ There are combination planting sticks and cleaning wands available from Hagen.

Your best investment is a good book. You really should study about aquariums and fishes BEFORE you get involved. If you can, buy the book so you can have it available for constant reference. Otherwise visit your local library or rent a book from your local pet shop. ▶

Male Bettas cannot be kept together or they will fight and tear each others fins apart. Yet keeping males close to each other produces fin flares that are magnificent to watch. This is possible with a Hagen Betta Barracks. ➥

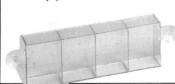

PUMPS & FILTERS

Each aquarium can adequately maintain about one inch of fish for each gallon of water—that means ten small fishes in a ten-gallon tank. This usually does not present a satisfactory arrangement as most people want more life in their aquarium. To increase the aquarium's capacity to sustain fish life it is necessary to aerate the water, thereby adding oxygen and removing carbon dioxide. This is done with a pump. A filter, always activated by a pump, removes harmful chemicals, debris and even toxic gases. Therefore, a pump and filter are necessities that should be bought when you buy your original tank set up.

Hagen has an air pump that is battery powered. This is useful for emergencies or when taking your fish on a long trip.

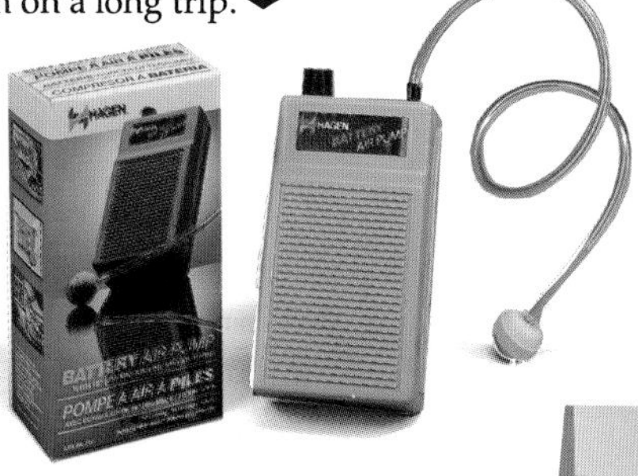

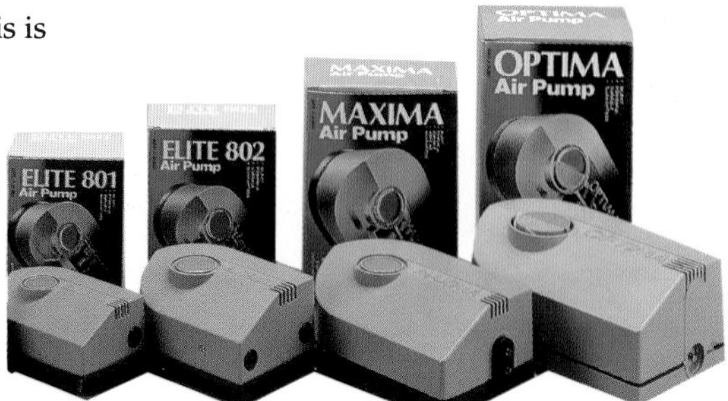

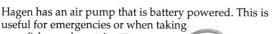

Special air pumps running via vibrating membranes are available in at least 4 different sizes. Photo by Hagen.

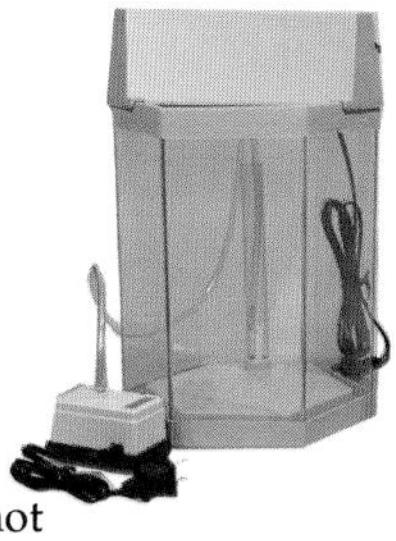

Air pumps running small inside filters must be matched. You don't want excessive air to interfere with the operation of the filter.

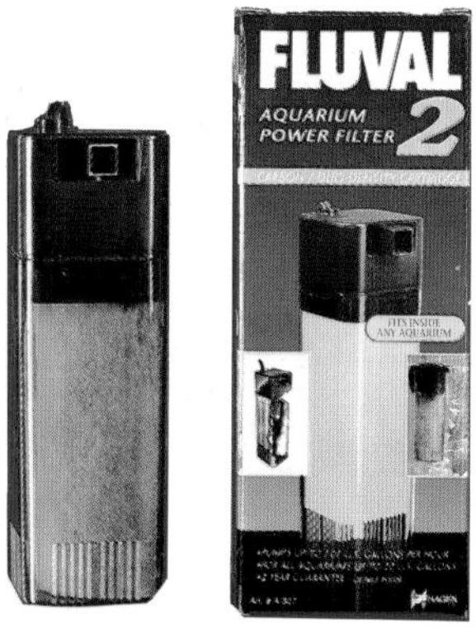

Never remove a submergible electrical pump (or heater) unless it is disconnected.

It's not how large the aquarium is that is important, but how DEEP it is, as depth creates back pressure and a more powerful pump is needed for deep tanks.

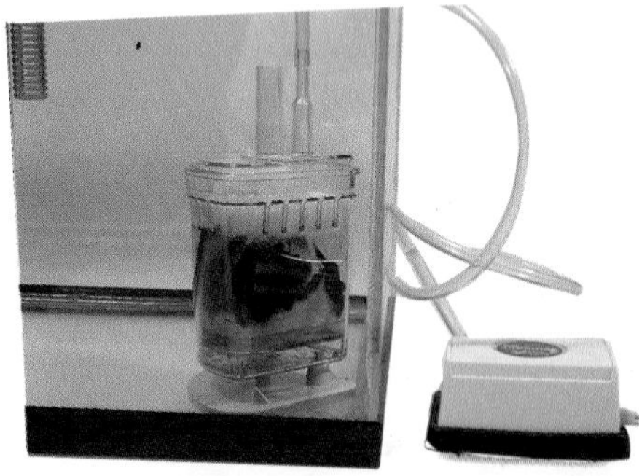

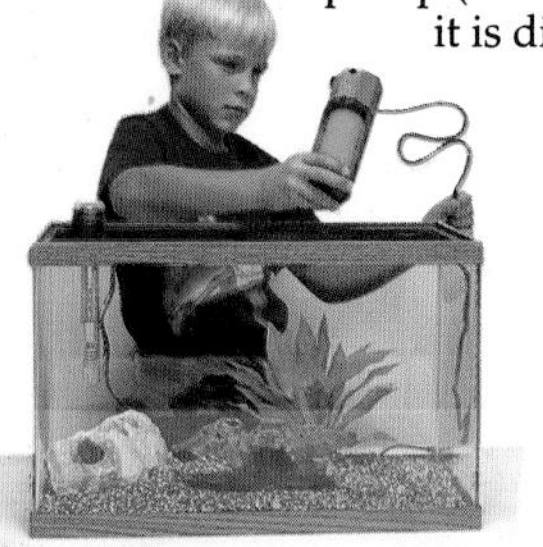

Hagen has a series of more powerful and adjustable pumps.

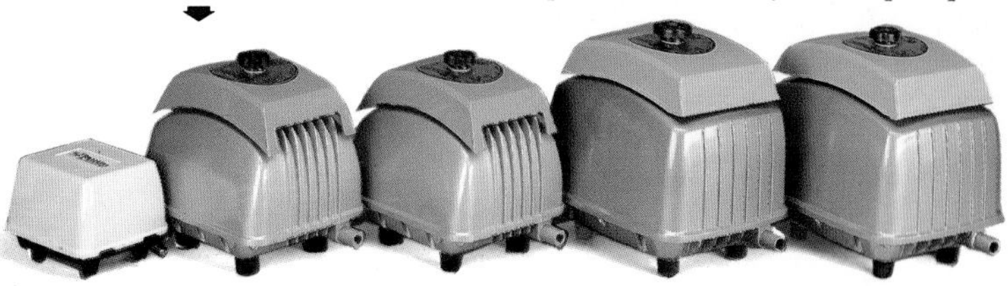

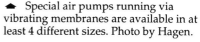

A new kind of filtration based upon bacterial activity plus mechanical filtration is called *WET-DRY* filtration. The Bio- Life Hagen is a good one which I have used successfully on a 20-gallon tank for over a year without changing water.

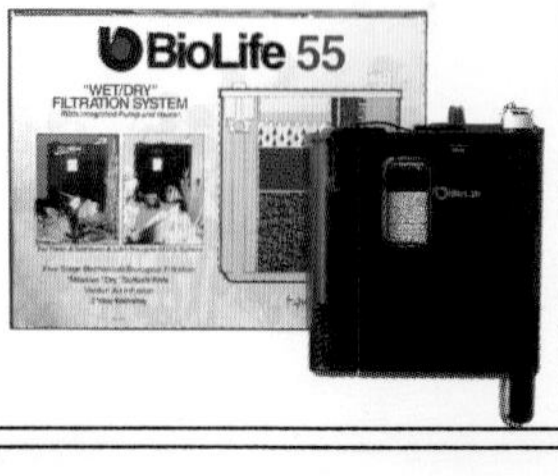

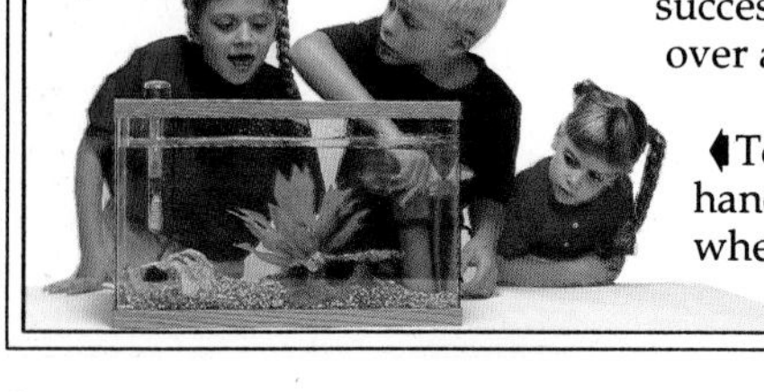

Teach your children to keep their hands out of the tank especially when electrical gadgets are alive.

Buy plastic tubing and cut it to the length you need to connect the filter to the air pump. ➛

◀ Locate the pump as close to the tank as possible and, if possible, above the tank to prevent siphoning of the water should the pump fail.

▶ There are many qualities in plastic tubing. The Hagen Silicone is the highest quality. Buy it in long lengths as it must be changed periodically.

➛ There are attachments and cartridges available for all power heads and under gravel filters. It can double the filtering capacity of your pump/filter.

Airline tubing comes in various lengths and qualities. You need about 20 feet to set up the usual aquarium. ➛

Gang valves help you adjust the air pump to various outlets in filters and ornaments. ▶

➛ There are many filters that accommodate the addition of filter charcoal or activated carbon. You should use activated carbon and change it weekly.

Activated carbon removes harmful gases like carbon dioxide, as well as medications that discolor the water. ▶

Poly wool is a filter material which physically removes suspended particles passing through the filter. It is necessary to change or wash the wool every week or so depending on the amount of debris accumulated. ▶

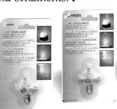

The Aqua-Clear Power Filter by Hagen can be charged with activated carbon and *poly* filter wool. ▶

UNDER GRAVEL FILTERS

Undergravel filters fit under the gravel and should cover the complete bottom. This is the lazy-man's filter since there is no carbon or wool to change, but it has limited effectiveness.

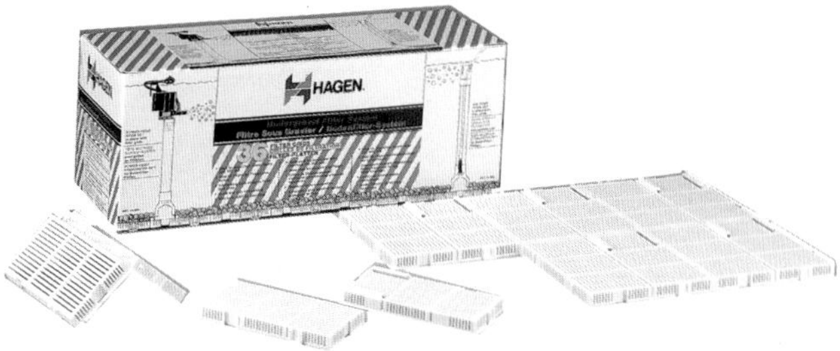

Hagen has a do-it-yourself undergravel filter kit. The squares interlock and each square is sturdy and self supported making it possible to use it again for a different size aquarium.

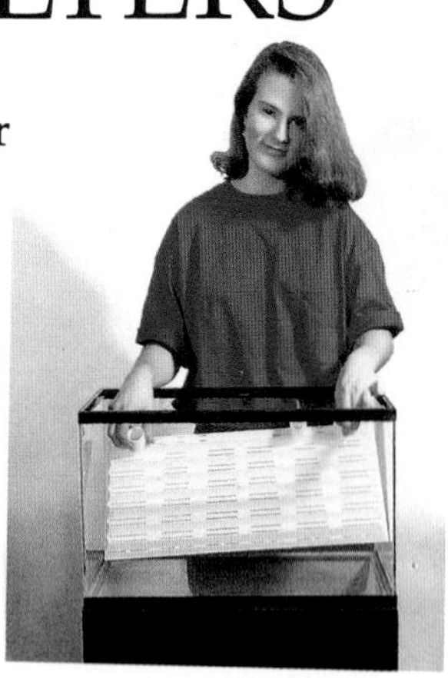

Undergravel filters should fit the bottom of the tank perfectly. The tank must be empty when it is fitted.

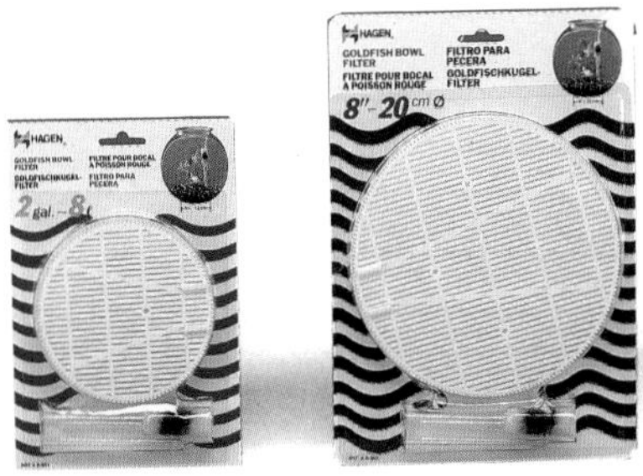

Hagen even makes undergravel filters for goldfish bowl or other round-bottomed aquariums.

The aerating columns of the undergravel filters should not rise above the top of the tank.

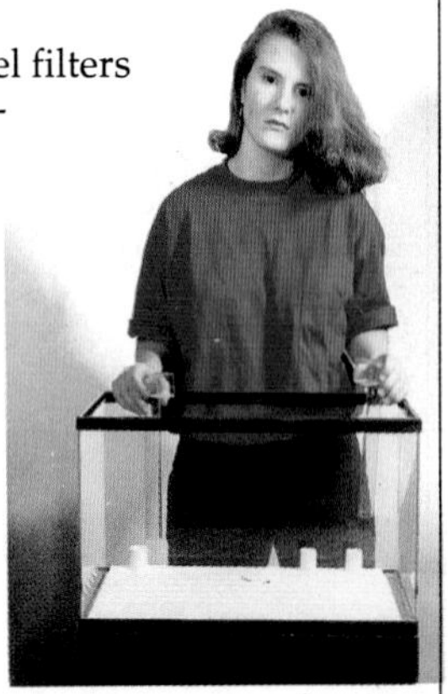

Undergravel filters should be equipped with aerating columns like the ClearFlow by Hagen.

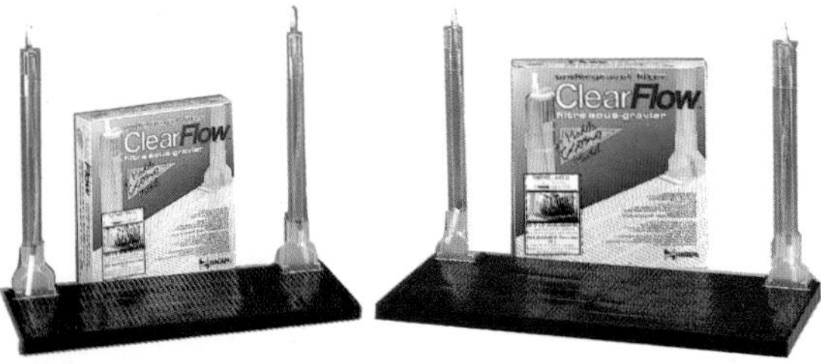

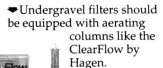

Once the undergravel filter is in place with the aerating columns set, the gravel can be added. The gravel should be about two inches deep to provide proper filtration.

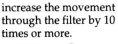

Powerheads attached to the aerating column can increase the movement through the filter by 10 times or more.

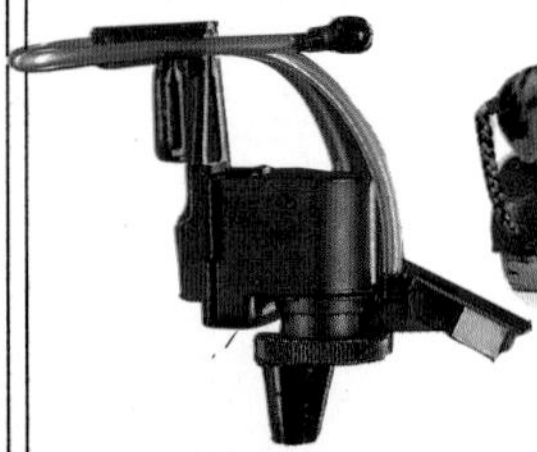

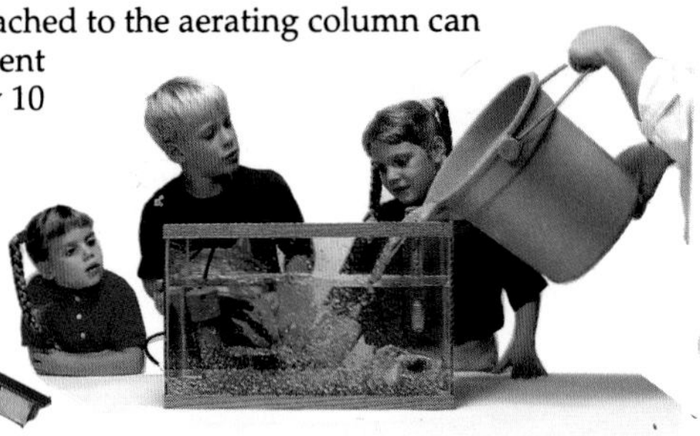

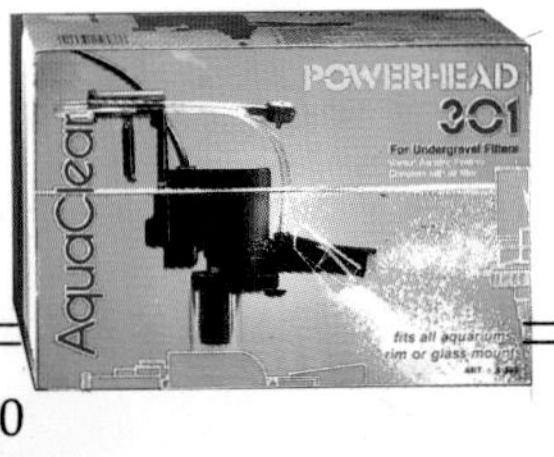

Don't ruin everything by adding water to a set up aquarium in a vigorous manner which uproots the plants and disturbs the gravel.

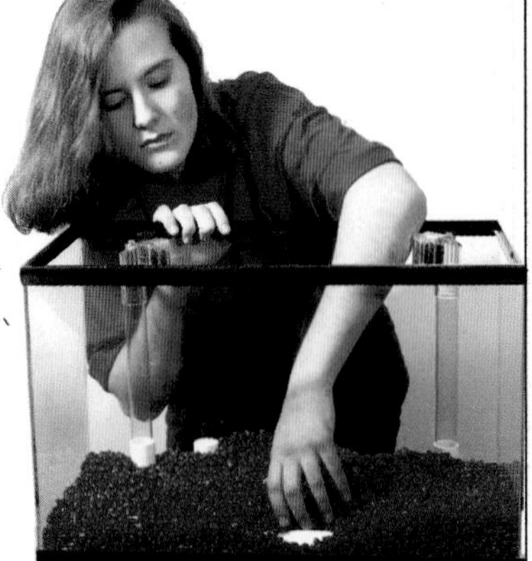

HEATERS

Aquarium heaters are a necessity in most temperate or frigid zones. Aquarium heaters come in sizes measured by watts, usually in steps of 25 or 50 watts. In the average home, a heater of about 5 watts per gallon capacity of the aquarium is suitable. A good heater can hold the water to within a 3°F fluctuation, which is just fine with fishes because this same thing happens in nature... cold at night and warm during the day.

Stick-On Thermometers by Hagen attach to the outside glass of the aquarium. ▶

▶ The Thermal Pre-set Aquarium Heaters range from 50 watts to 300 watts. In large tanks it is best to use two heaters in case one fails.

This outside heater attaches to the rim of the aquarium. The top must be kept dry and out of the water.

The Hagen Compact line of heaters is outside adjustable. Ask your dealer for the heater you should have. ▶

Hagen makes a Solar Electronic line of submersible heaters. ◀

The Hagen Radiant Heaters are designed for smaller aquariums. ▶

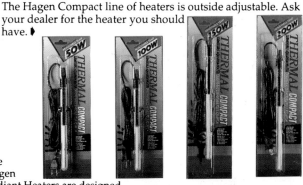

A floating thermometer. ◀

A stick-on thermometer. ◀

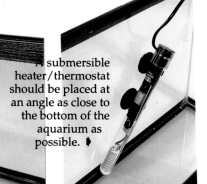

A normal heater attaches to the rim of the tank. ▶

A submersible heater/thermostat should be placed at an angle as close to the bottom of the aquarium as possible. ▶

FOODS AND FEEDING

Fishes convert about 30% of the food they eat into body size. This formula holds true only when a fish has more food offered than he can eat at that moment. Obviously food laying in an aquarium rots and fouls the water, so growing fishes should be fed as frequently as possible, but in small quantities. The quantity should be eaten within two minutes or you have overfed. Living foods are great for all fishes, but even a total diet of living foods is not balanced. If you can offer brine shrimp or Daphnia once a day and dry foods the rest of the time, you will be successful. *Vary the dry foods as much as possible.* Freeze-dried foods are the best of all dried foods, but they are also expensive.

← Nutrafin Staple Food is suitable for the daily dry food ration.

The most ideal aquarium fish food is living brine shrimp. The eggs from San Francisco Bay Brand are the best by far. ➡

← Frozen foods are wonderful for your fishes. Get a package of each kind of live food, keep it in the freezer until needed, and then break off a piece. The piece should be put into your net and rinsed under warm (not hot) water until the foods melt and soften. Then they can be offered to the fishes.

Nutrafin Red Grubs is a unique food produced by Hagen of Canada. Hagen has a rich variety of dried foods which should be used in your normal food rotation. The dried foods should be soaked in water for half an hour so it falls to the bottom where bottom feeding and mid-level feeders can get to them. ➡

◀ Bulk foods are available in pails and other larger sized containers.

It seems rather obvious that nets are necessary to catch living fishes; they are also necessary to remove dead fishes which may have decayed a bit and are not for the squeamish to handle without a net. Nets should be made from soft, porous nylon. The pores should be large enough to allow the net to be pulled through the water without back pressure. The pocket of the net should be as deep as possible so that a netted fish cannot swim or jump out easily.

A net should have a handle that is long enough to capture a fish at the bottom of the opposite side—the hypotenuse of the triangle formed by the front glass, the surface of the gravel and the net (If you remember your Geometry!). ◄

◄ To catch a fish comfortably remove the top cover or canopy and view the fish *from the side*, not from the top as shown here.

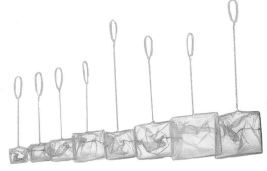

◄ Nets are available with different size mesh pockets and different length handles. Get the one that suits your needs. You do need a small net for a small tank and a large net for a large tank.

EASY CATCH NET

HAGEN

A small net is required to fit inside the top of the goldfish bowl. ►

Catching a fish with a small net while viewing from above is impossible. You have to look through the sides of the aquarium to catch the fish. ►

◄ A small net is needed to catch the fish in the goldfish bowl, but the same net is too small for the 10-gallon tank.

COMMUNITY AQUARIUM

◄ The problem with large aquariums with so many plants is that the fishes do not produce enough carbon dioxide to assist the plants in photosynthesis. It is the process of photosynthesis that allows the plants to manufacture food for growth and sustenance. Tetra makes suitable kits for supplying carbon dioxide to the aquarium.

◄ This wonderful planted community aquarium houses a full complement of fishes. The equipment used, water conditions and maintenance data are outlined below.

DATA

Water temperature: 76°F.
Tank dimensions: 48 x 24 x 24 in., all-glass tank.
Lighting: 2 x 30-watt bulbs and 2 x 15-watt bulbs; daily illumination period 12 hours.
Influence of daylight: Up to midday.
Substrate: Coarse beach or river sand.
Filtration: External filtration system.
Water changes: 1/3 of total volume once per week.
Heating: 200-watt heater.
Fertilizer: Addition of plant fertilizer, depending upon condition of plants.
Water quality: pH 6.8.
Carbonate hardness: 6° DH.
Carbon dioxide in solution: 10 mg.

Piranhas are steeped in legend. Separating fact from legend can sometimes be a challenge, but suffice it to say that they have a largely undeserved reputation for bloodthirstiness. Piranhas are carnivores, but so are most fishes. Pacus and Metynnis are closely related to Piranhas but less dangerous.

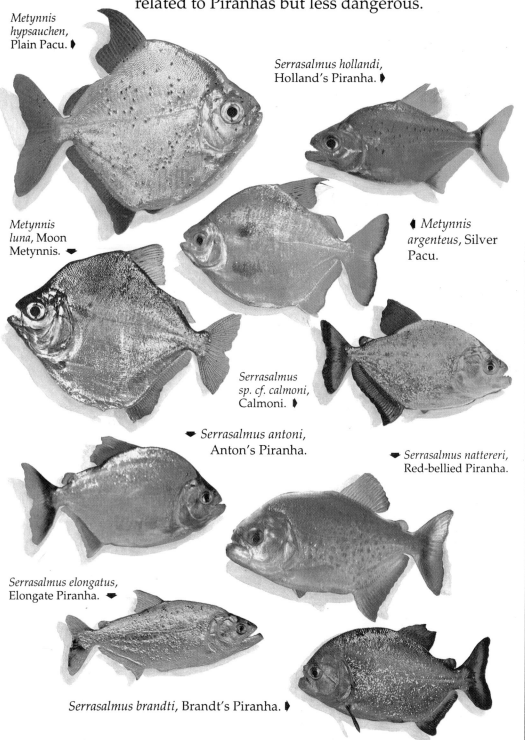

Metynnis hypsauchen, Plain Pacu. ▶

Serrasalmus hollandi, Holland's Piranha. ▶

Metynnis luna, Moon Metynnis. ◀

◀ *Metynnis argenteus,* Silver Pacu.

Serrasalmus sp. cf. calmoni, Calmoni. ▶

◀ *Serrasalmus antoni,* Anton's Piranha.

◀ *Serrasalmus nattereri,* Red-bellied Piranha.

Serrasalmus elongatus, Elongate Piranha. ◀

Serrasalmus brandti, Brandt's Piranha. ▶

TETRAS

Tetras, or characins, are schooling fish that don't thrive when kept alone or with only one or two of their kind. They are very alert and have a keen sense of hearing. They are the first to find new food in the aquarium. They are also the first to sense danger, which sends them into tight, protective schools. Tetras are hardy fish that prefer clear, well-aerated moving water. Peat-filtered water in a planted tank usually leads to spawning.

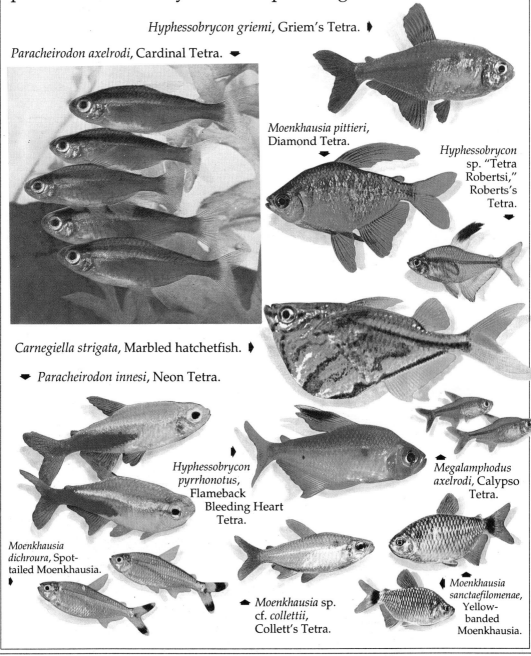

Hyphessobrycon griemi, Griem's Tetra. ▶

Paracheirodon axelrodi, Cardinal Tetra. ➡

Moenkhausia pittieri, Diamond Tetra. ⬇

Hyphessobrycon sp. "Tetra Robertsi," Roberts's Tetra. ⬇

Carnegiella strigata, Marbled hatchetfish. ▶

➡ *Paracheirodon innesi*, Neon Tetra.

Hyphessobrycon pyrrhonotus, Flameback Bleeding Heart Tetra.

Megalamphodus axelrodi, Calypso Tetra.

Moenkhausia dichroura, Spot-tailed Moenkhausia. ▶

⬅ *Moenkhausia* sp. cf. *collettii*, Collett's Tetra.

Moenkhausia sanctaefilomenae, Yellow-banded Moenkhausia.

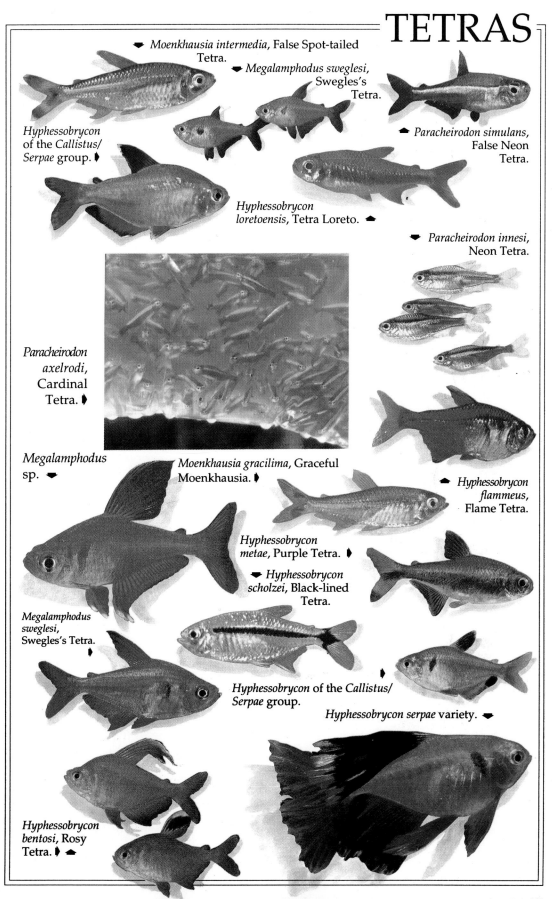

Moenkhausia intermedia, False Spot-tailed Tetra.

Megalamphodus sweglesi, Swegles's Tetra.

Hyphessobrycon of the *Callistus/ Serpae* group.

Paracheirodon simulans, False Neon Tetra.

Hyphessobrycon loretoensis, Tetra Loreto.

Paracheirodon innesi, Neon Tetra.

Paracheirodon axelrodi, Cardinal Tetra.

Megalamphodus sp.

Moenkhausia gracilima, Graceful Moenkhausia.

Hyphessobrycon flammeus, Flame Tetra.

Hyphessobrycon metae, Purple Tetra.

Hyphessobrycon scholzei, Black-lined Tetra.

Megalamphodus sweglesi, Swegles's Tetra.

Hyphessobrycon of the *Callistus/ Serpae* group.

Hyphessobrycon serpae variety.

Hyphessobrycon bentosi, Rosy Tetra.

BARBS

Barbs, or cyprinids, add action and color to the aquarium. Busy fishes, the barbs are always on the look-out for a stray morsel of food or a nip of a fin. Many of the barbs like to school, and show their best colors and behavior when kept with six or more of their own kind.

Capoeta tetrazona,
Tiger Barb.

Barbodes aff. *binotatus,*
Spotted Barb. ▶

Puntius bandula,
Banded Barb.

Capoeta tetrazona,
Tiger Barb, male. ◀

Capoeta hulstaerti,
Butterfly Barb. ◀

Capoeta tetrazona,
Tiger Barb, female. ▶

Puntius narayani,
Sri Lankan Two-spot Barb. ◀

Capoeta semifasciolatus, Thin-banded Barb. ▶

◀ *Puntius titteya,* Cherry Barb.

Puntius conchonius,
Rosy Barb.

18

BARBS

Capoeta oligolepis, Checkerboard Barb.

Puntius nigrofasciatus, Black Ruby Barb.

Puntius sachsi, Gold Barb.

Capoeta tetrazona, Tiger Barb.

Puntius ticto, Tic-Tac-Toe Barb.

Puntius conchonius, Rosy Barb.

Puntius amphibius, Big-scale Barb.

Capoeta arulius, Longfin Barb.

Puntius conchonius, Rosy Barb.

Puntius filamentosus, Black-spot Filament Barb.

CICHLIDS

Dwarf Cichlids are all under four inches in length. They like planted tanks with some rock caves and driftwood. The water should be soft, slightly acidic, and have a temperature of between 72 and 75°F. Most Dwarf Cichlids are very peaceful and should be kept with non-aggressive tank mates. (Dwarf Cichlids shown on this and facing page, non-dwarf Cichlid species on pages 22 and 23.)

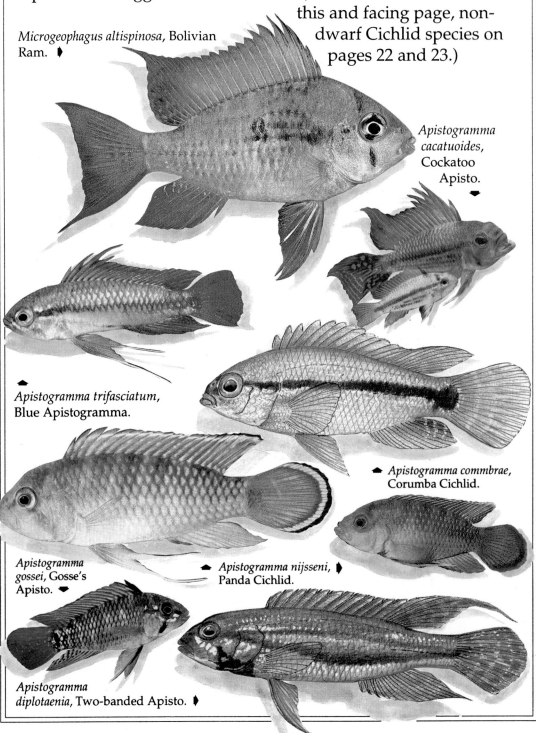

Microgeophagus altispinosa, Bolivian Ram. ▶

Apistogramma cacatuoides, Cockatoo Apisto. ◆

Apistogramma trifasciatum, Blue Apistogramma.

◆ *Apistogramma commbrae*, Corumba Cichlid.

Apistogramma gossei, Gosse's Apisto. ◆

◆ *Apistogramma nijsseni*, ▶ Panda Cichlid.

Apistogramma diplotaenia, Two-banded Apisto. ▶

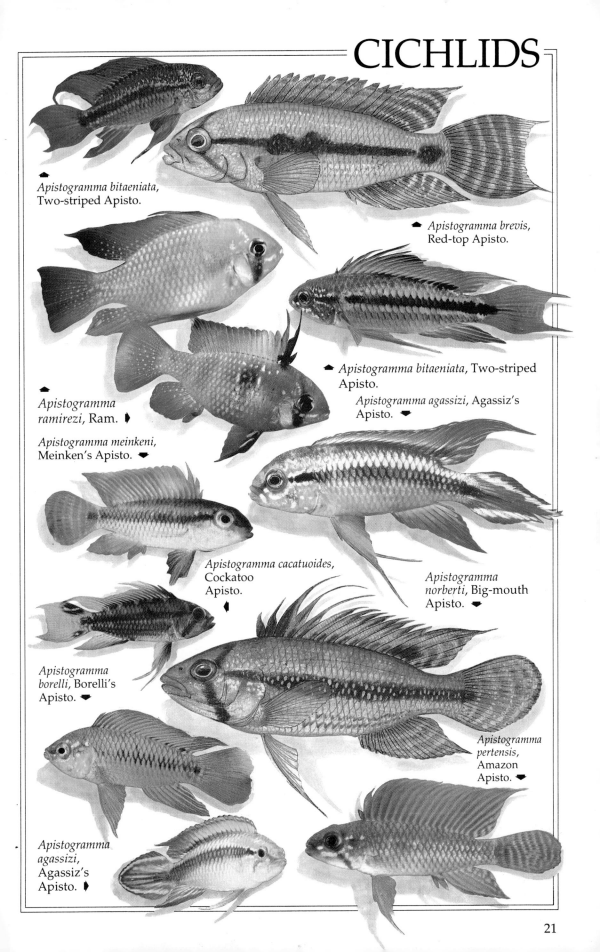

Apistogramma bitaeniata,
Two-striped Apisto.

Apistogramma brevis,
Red-top Apisto.

Apistogramma bitaeniata, Two-striped
Apisto.

Apistogramma agassizi, Agassiz's
Apisto.

*Apistogramma
ramirezi,* Ram.

Apistogramma meinkeni,
Meinken's Apisto.

Apistogramma cacatuoides,
Cockatoo
Apisto.

*Apistogramma
norberti,* Big-mouth
Apisto.

*Apistogramma
borelli,* Borelli's
Apisto.

*Apistogramma
pertensis,*
Amazon
Apisto.

*Apistogramma
agassizi,*
Agassiz's
Apisto.

CICHLIDS

Herichthys nigrofasciatum, Convict Cichlid, an unusual color morph.

Herichthys pearsei, Pearse's Cichlid.

Cichlasoma amazonarum, Amazon Cichlid.

Herichthys nigrofasciatum, Convict Cichlid, normally colored variety.

Herichthys octofasciatum, Jack Dempsey.

Cichlasoma portalegrensis, Port Cichlid.

Cichlasoma dimerus, Green Port Cichlid.

Herichthys synspilum, Redheaded Cichlid.

Herichthys rhytisma, Spangled Alfari.

Cichla ocellaris, Peacock Cichlid.

Astronotus ocellatus, Oscar.

Astronotus crassipinnis, Pantanal Oscar.

Astronotus ocellatus, Oscar.

Astronotus ocellatus, Oscar.

Astronotus ocellatus, Oscar.

Astronotus ocellatus, Oscar, albino.

Herichthys nebuliferum, Smoky Cichlid.

Astronotus ocellatus, Oscar.

Herichthys salvini, Salvini.

Herichthys spilurum, Blue-eyed Cichlid.

Herichthys regani, Regan's Cichlid.

Herichthys nicaraguensis, Spilotum.

Herichthys salvini, Salvini.

RAINBOWS AND GOBIES

Australia and New Guinea were once connected, so we expect to find similar fishes on both islands...and we do. These are mostly fishes of the genera *Melanotaenia* and *Hypseleotris*. Their double dorsal fin tells us they are derived from salt water and are probably tolerant of cool temperatures as well. These are very highly colored fishes, easy to breed and simple to care for. Many of them look alike as they go through various color changes due to age, feed, or sexual activity. Fortunately they rarely fight amongst themselves or with other fishes. They also don't eat either their own eggs or the eggs of their tankmates. They thrive on dry food as well as living foods. All fishes should get some live foods from time to time. These fishes are usually found in fast-moving mountain streams so they do need heavily oxygenated water which is unheated. Heated water cannot hold enough oxygen for them. They do NOT thrive under pet shop conditions, so don't be discouraged when you see them lacking color in a pet shop aquarium.

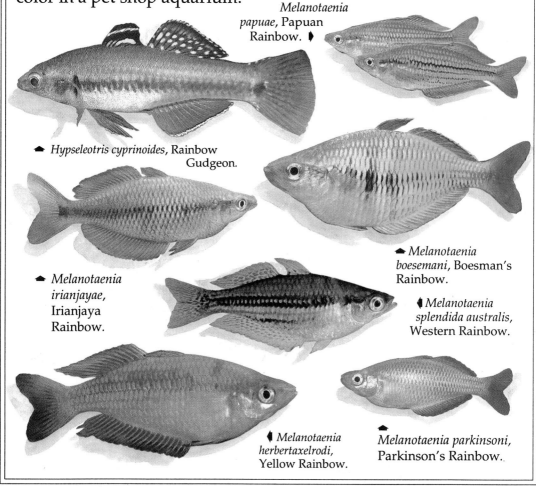

Melanotaenia papuae, Papuan Rainbow. ▶

◀ *Hypseleotris cyprinoides*, Rainbow Gudgeon.

◀ *Melanotaenia irianjayae*, Irianjaya Rainbow.

◀ *Melanotaenia boesemani*, Boesman's Rainbow.

◀ *Melanotaenia splendida australis*, Western Rainbow.

◀ *Melanotaenia herbertaxelrodi*, Yellow Rainbow.

Melanotaenia parkinsoni, Parkinson's Rainbow.

RAINBOWS AND GOBIES

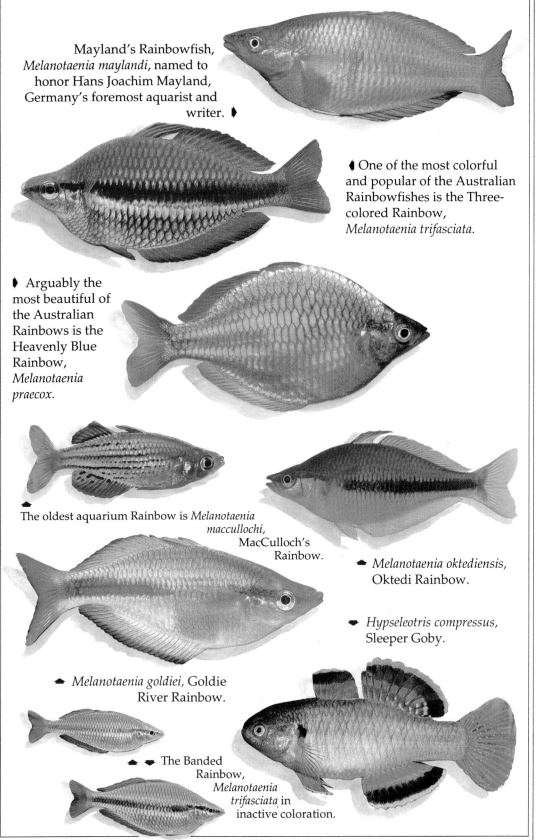

Mayland's Rainbowfish, *Melanotaenia maylandi*, named to honor Hans Joachim Mayland, Germany's foremost aquarist and writer. ▶

◀ One of the most colorful and popular of the Australian Rainbowfishes is the Three-colored Rainbow, *Melanotaenia trifasciata*.

▶ Arguably the most beautiful of the Australian Rainbows is the Heavenly Blue Rainbow, *Melanotaenia praecox*.

The oldest aquarium Rainbow is *Melanotaenia maccullochi*, MacCulloch's Rainbow.

◀ *Melanotaenia oktediensis*, Oktedi Rainbow.

◀ *Hypseleotris compressus*, Sleeper Goby.

◀ *Melanotaenia goldiei*, Goldie River Rainbow.

◀ ▶ The Banded Rainbow, *Melanotaenia trifasciata* in inactive coloration.

BETTAS

Until banned in about 1965, the Thai people would fight cocks, fishes and people in ways that were strange to the world. Chickens (cocks) would have razor-sharp knives attached to their feet. Fish were bred to fight until one fish gave up. These fish were called *Siamese Fighting Fish*, or *Betta splendens* as they are known scientifically. The males have very long fins and they fight every other male they see until one runs away and hides. In a small aquarium the loser would be bitten to death in many cases. Females, too, may be attacked if they are not ready for spawning but have come to the attention of the male. Females may be kept together without any difficulty. Males must be isolated from each other in special compartments called *Betta Barracks*.

This is a Red Betta female, swollen with eggs.

This color is called *Cambodian*, but the scientific name is still *Betta splendens*.

The ultimate creation is the all-black Siamese Fighting Fish. This magnificent specimen has blue as well as black.

Modified Cambodian Betta. This is a rare color.

Blue female Betta. Note the shorter dorsal.

This is a hybrid between *Betta splendens* and *Betta imbellis*.

The Golden Split-tail Betta, sometimes called a Peach Split-tail.

The lovely Violet Betta.

26

BETTAS

This is a beautiful Black Betta. Black is a difficult color to breed in Bettas. Almost any solid color is difficult; colors are usually adorned with other colors. ◗

← A close-up of a bubblenest with the *Betta* fry clinging to the bubbles. Bettas make bubblenests and spit their eggs into the nest of foam. These fish are easy to spawn. Read a book about BREEDING AQUARIUM FISHES.

◗ A champion quality Blue Turquoise Betta.

← A poorly colored *Betta splendens*, but with very long fins.

Cornflower Blue Betta. ⬇

◗ A Black Betta male flaring his gill covers.

← Blue/black *Betta imbellis*.

← A female *Betta splendens*.

← A cross between a *Betta imbellis* and a *Betta splendens*.

A short-bodied Brown/black male *Betta splendens*.

◗ A very young *Betta splendens*.

GOLDFISH

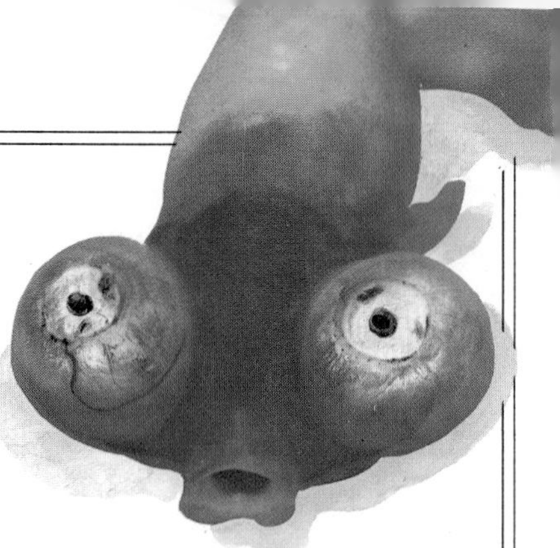

Goldfish are hardy, long-lived pets. They are not tropical fish but are what are called temperate fish. This simply means that they are found in cool water. You won't need a heater in the aquarium when you keep Goldfish.

Celestial Goldfish. The Celestial Goldfish always stare toward the heavens, hence the name "Celestial."

Common Goldfish. Common Goldfish are inexpensive, attractive, and very hardy—perfect starter fish for newcomers to the hobby.

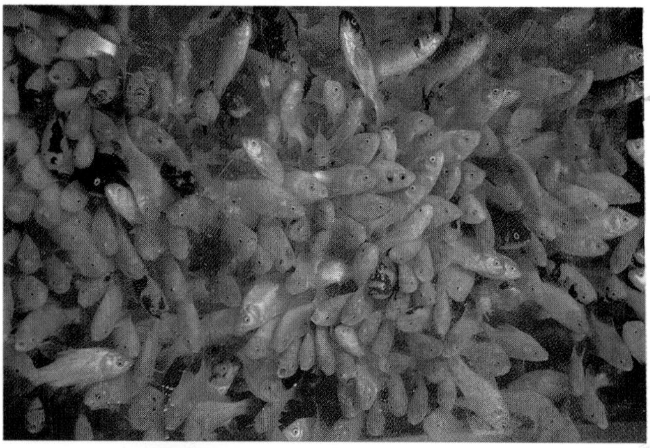

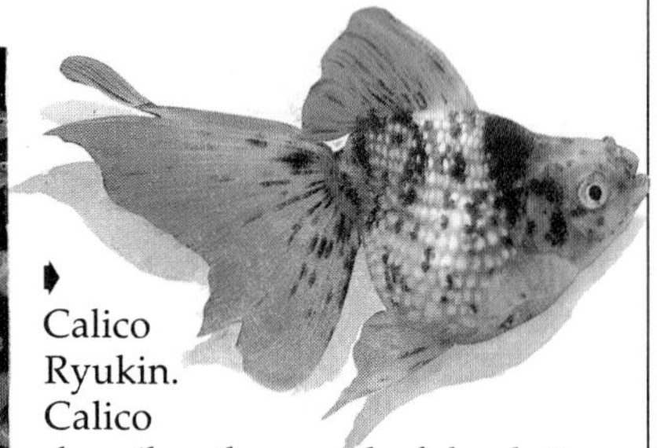

Calico Ryukin. Calico describes the wonderful palette of colors on these fish, no two of which are exactly alike.

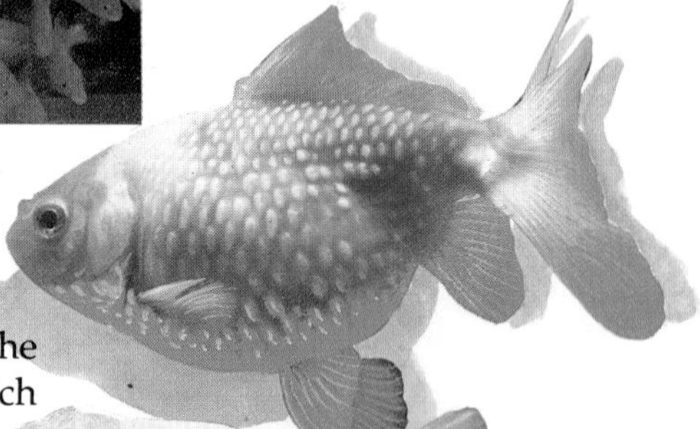

Pearlscale. Each scale is raised and reflects light like the pearls for which this fish is named.

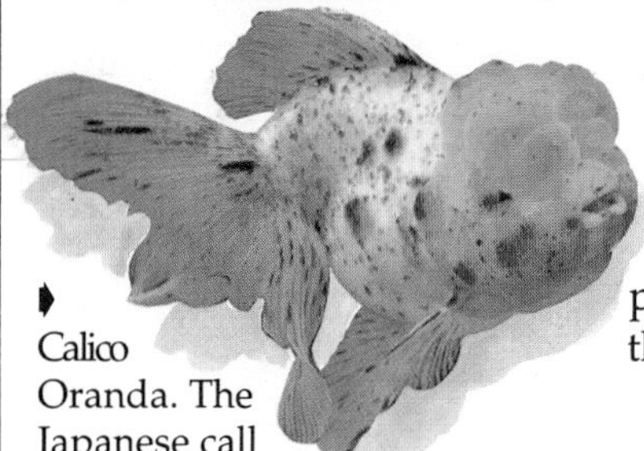

Calico Oranda. The Japanese call this fish an Azumanishiki.

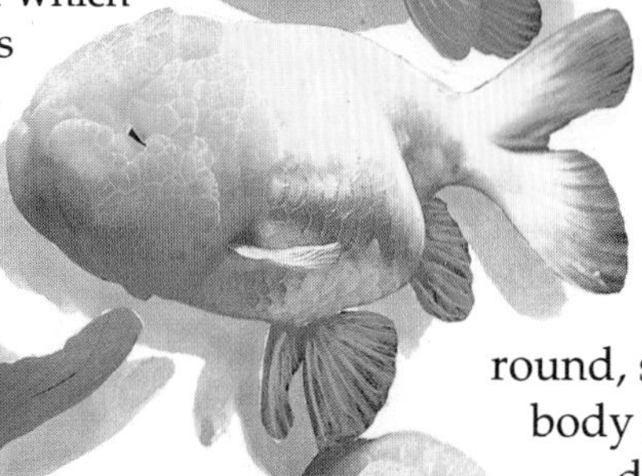

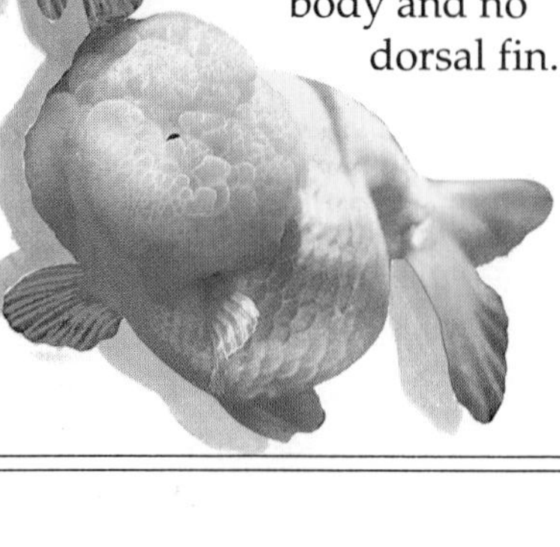

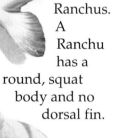

Ranchus. A Ranchu has a round, squat body and no dorsal fin.

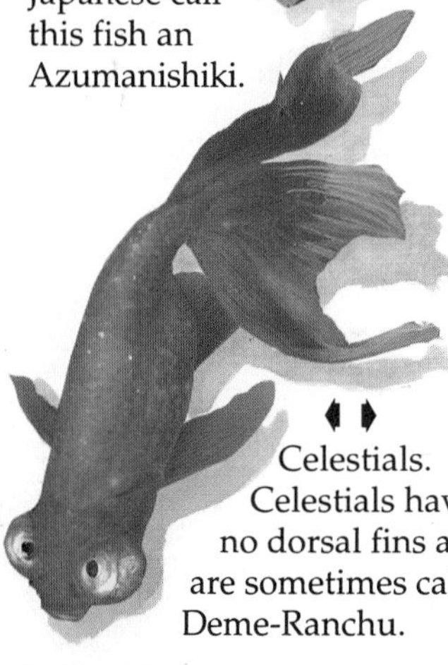

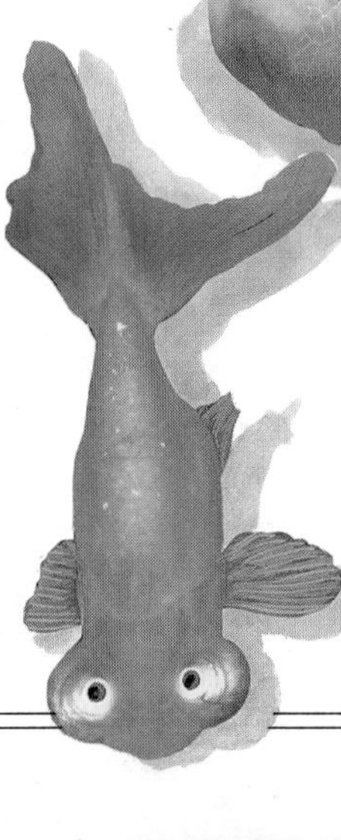

Celestials. Celestials have no dorsal fins and are sometimes called Deme-Ranchu.

Oranda. The headgrowth on Orandas increases with maturity.

Veiltail Oranda. Long-finned Goldfish need very clean water to prevent damage to the fins.

Oranda. Do not keep Orandas with fast-swimming fish as they are too slow to compete for food.

White Redcap Oranda. The contrast of white and red makes this a magnificent fish.

Redcap Oranda. The Redcap is one of the most popular of the Orandas.

Calico Oranda. The red in Calicos will intensify with a diet high in vegetable matter.

Bubble-eye Goldfish. The eye-sacs are filled with water.

Bubble-eye Goldfish. If the bubble is damaged it will grow back, but not as magnificently as the original.

GOLDFISH

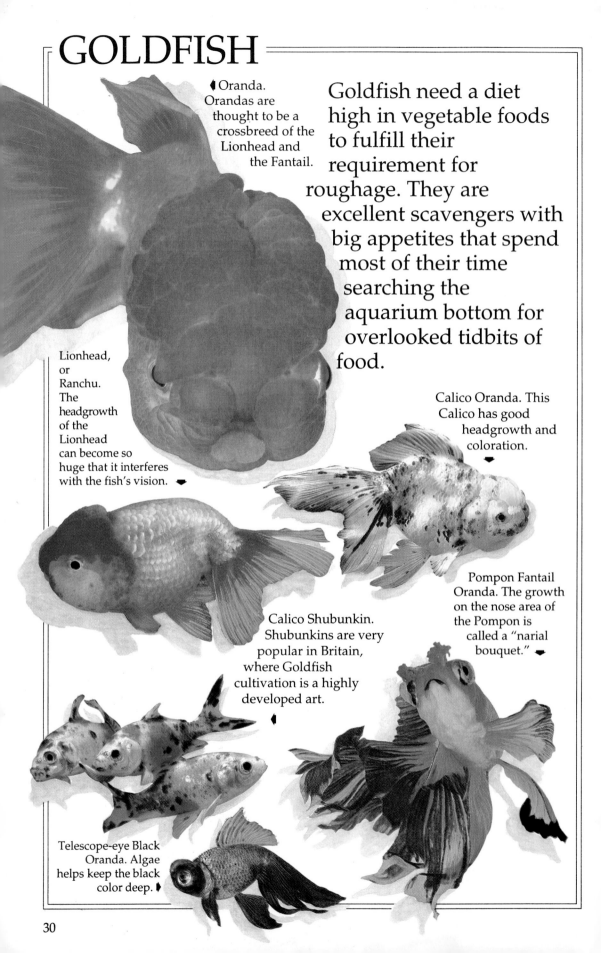

◀ Oranda. Orandas are thought to be a crossbreed of the Lionhead and the Fantail.

Goldfish need a diet high in vegetable foods to fulfill their requirement for roughage. They are excellent scavengers with big appetites that spend most of their time searching the aquarium bottom for overlooked tidbits of food.

Lionhead, or Ranchu. The headgrowth of the Lionhead can become so huge that it interferes with the fish's vision. ➡

Calico Oranda. This Calico has good headgrowth and coloration. ◀

Pompon Fantail Oranda. The growth on the nose area of the Pompon is called a "narial bouquet." ➡

Calico Shubunkin. Shubunkins are very popular in Britain, where Goldfish cultivation is a highly developed art. ◀

Telescope-eye Black Oranda. Algae helps keep the black color deep. ▶

GOLDFISH

Ryukin. ▶

▶ Black Moor Goldfish.

Lionhead, or Ranchu. The size and shape of the head-growth depends on genetics, nutrition, and water quality.

Ryukins. Many Ryukins become more colorful as they age. ▼

Pearl-scale Oranda. If a pearled scale is lost, the new scale will be normal, not pearl. ▼

Veiltail Goldfish.

◀ Redcap Oranda.

Jikin. The Jikin is usually bicolored. ▼

Oranda. The Oranda always has a dorsal fin. ▼

Pearlscale Oranda. ▼

◀ Black Oranda.

▼ Oranda.

Chocolate Oranda. ▼

The Chinese Lionhead.

◀ Calico Telescope-eye.

Bubble-eye Goldfish. This fish could have been crossed with a Celestial in an effort to combine features of both. ▶

LIVEBEARERS

LIVEBEARERS are the most popular of aquarium fishes. They are easy to keep, easy to breed and relatively inexpensive. Most of them are raised in Florida, Singapore, Hong Kong and Malaysia. Almost everybody starts their tropical fish hobby with a Guppy, Molly, Platy or Swordtail. With any of these fishes, the males and females are easy to differentiate. All have fry about once a month and all eat their own fry under most circumstances. Pet shops sell breeding traps to protect the fry.

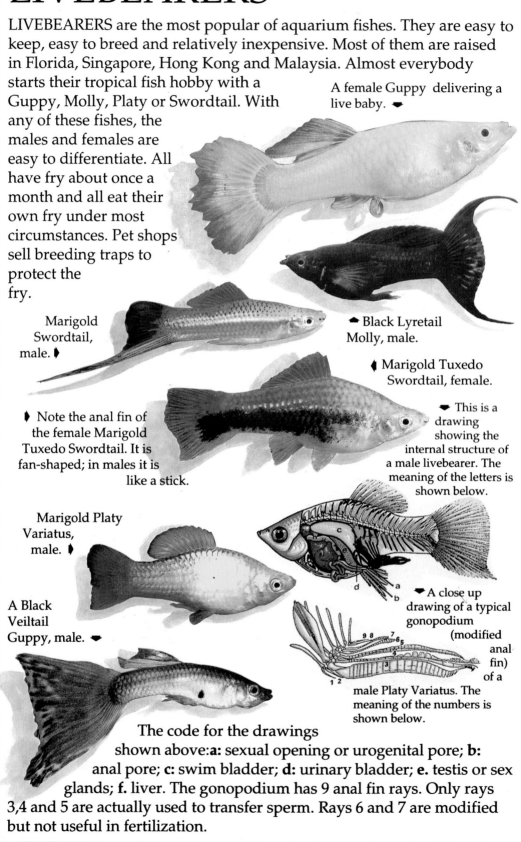

A female Guppy delivering a live baby. ➡

Marigold Swordtail, male. ▸

◂ Black Lyretail Molly, male.

◂ Marigold Tuxedo Swordtail, female.

▸ Note the anal fin of the female Marigold Tuxedo Swordtail. It is fan-shaped; in males it is like a stick.

➡ This is a drawing showing the internal structure of a male livebearer. The meaning of the letters is shown below.

Marigold Platy Variatus, male. ▸

A Black Veiltail Guppy, male. ➡

➡ A close up drawing of a typical gonopodium (modified anal fin) of a male Platy Variatus. The meaning of the numbers is shown below.

The code for the drawings shown above: **a:** sexual opening or urogenital pore; **b:** anal pore; **c:** swim bladder; **d:** urinary bladder; **e.** testis or sex glands; **f.** liver. The gonopodium has 9 anal fin rays. Only rays 3,4 and 5 are actually used to transfer sperm. Rays 6 and 7 are modified but not useful in fertilization.

SWORDTAILS always seem to have a small or large sword-like extension to their tail fin. They did not get their name *swordtail* from this characteristic. Their old scientific name was *Xiphophorus* which means *sword-bearer*. But the name was used to describe the modified anal fins of the males as being *like a sword*.

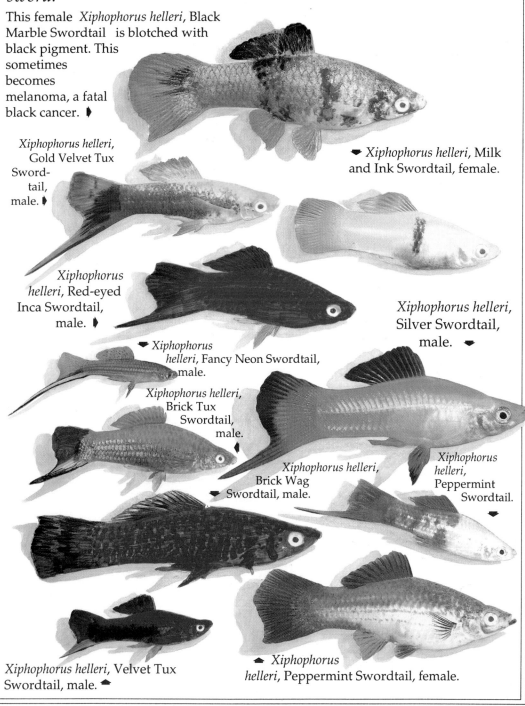

This female *Xiphophorus helleri*, Black Marble Swordtail is blotched with black pigment. This sometimes becomes melanoma, a fatal black cancer. ▶

Xiphophorus helleri, Gold Velvet Tux Sword- tail, male. ▶

➡ *Xiphophorus helleri*, Milk and Ink Swordtail, female.

Xiphophorus helleri, Red-eyed Inca Swordtail, male. ▶

➡ *Xiphophorus helleri*, Fancy Neon Swordtail, male.

Xiphophorus helleri, Silver Swordtail, male. ➡

Xiphophorus helleri, Brick Tux Swordtail, male. ▲

Xiphophorus helleri, Brick Wag Swordtail, male.

Xiphophorus helleri, Peppermint Swordtail. ▼

Xiphophorus helleri, Velvet Tux Swordtail, male. ◀

▲ *Xiphophorus helleri*, Peppermint Swordtail, female.

SWORDTAILS

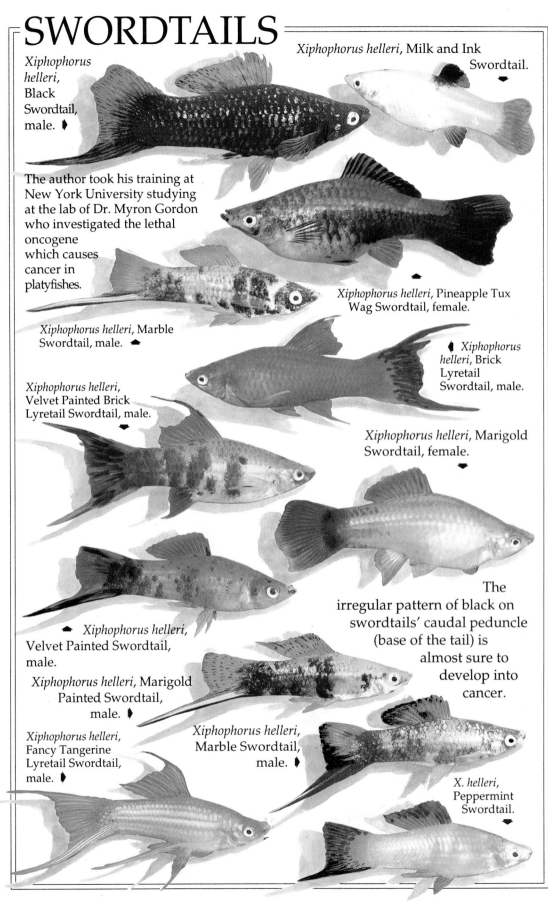

Xiphophorus helleri, Black Swordtail, male.

Xiphophorus helleri, Milk and Ink Swordtail.

The author took his training at New York University studying at the lab of Dr. Myron Gordon who investigated the lethal oncogene which causes cancer in platyfishes.

Xiphophorus helleri, Pineapple Tux Wag Swordtail, female.

Xiphophorus helleri, Marble Swordtail, male.

Xiphophorus helleri, Velvet Painted Brick Lyretail Swordtail, male.

Xiphophorus helleri, Brick Lyretail Swordtail, male.

Xiphophorus helleri, Marigold Swordtail, female.

The irregular pattern of black on swordtails' caudal peduncle (base of the tail) is almost sure to develop into cancer.

Xiphophorus helleri, Velvet Painted Swordtail, male.

Xiphophorus helleri, Marigold Painted Swordtail, male.

Xiphophorus helleri, Fancy Tangerine Lyretail Swordtail, male.

Xiphophorus helleri, Marble Swordtail, male.

X. helleri, Peppermint Swordtail.

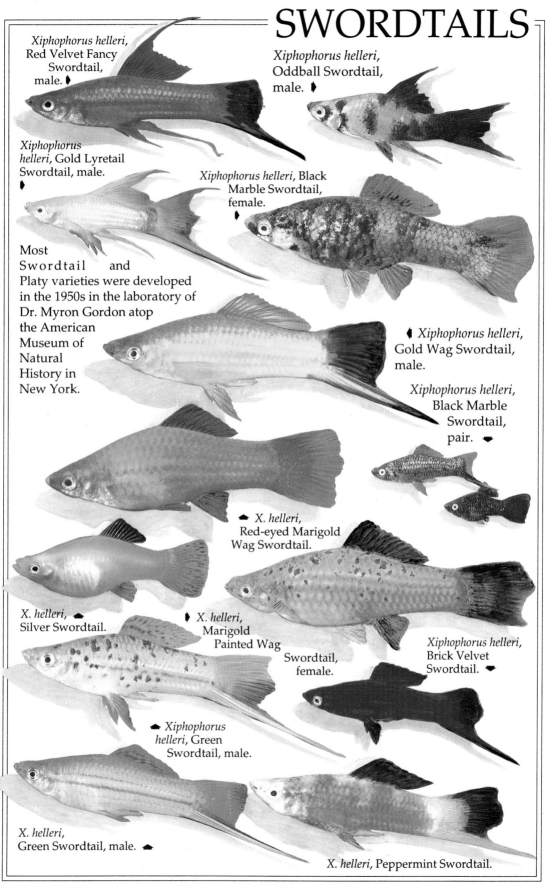

SWORDTAILS

Xiphophorus helleri, Red Velvet Fancy Swordtail, male. ▶

Xiphophorus helleri, Oddball Swordtail, male. ▶

Xiphophorus helleri, Gold Lyretail Swordtail, male. ▶

Xiphophorus helleri, Black Marble Swordtail, female. ▶

Most Swordtail and Platy varieties were developed in the 1950s in the laboratory of Dr. Myron Gordon atop the American Museum of Natural History in New York.

◀ *Xiphophorus helleri,* Gold Wag Swordtail, male.

Xiphophorus helleri, Black Marble Swordtail, pair. ◀

◀ *X. helleri,* Red-eyed Marigold Wag Swordtail.

X. helleri, Silver Swordtail. ◀

▶ *X. helleri,* Marigold Painted Wag Swordtail, female.

Xiphophorus helleri, Brick Velvet Swordtail. ◀

◀ *Xiphophorus helleri,* Green Swordtail, male.

X. helleri, Green Swordtail, male. ◀

X. helleri, Peppermint Swordtail.

PLATY VARIATUS

PLATY VARIATUS is the name given to a group of platies, most of which are of mixed parentage. There are, however, really Platy Variatus...real in the sense that they do exist in Nature. These fishes are called *Xiphophorus variatus*, previously known as *Platypoecilus variatus*, a name now discarded. It is easy to recognize these platies since they have the dorsal fin starting behind the hump on the back. They also have mixed colors, usually with special markings in the tail. The original females were colorless, but, after several inbreedings with the regular platies, *Xiphophorus maculatus*, the tuxedo pattern and color in the females was transferred to Platy Variatus.

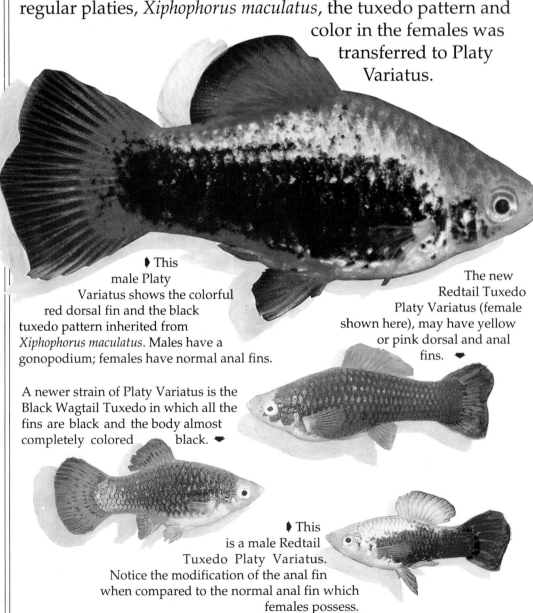

◗ This male Platy Variatus shows the colorful red dorsal fin and the black tuxedo pattern inherited from *Xiphophorus maculatus*. Males have a gonopodium; females have normal anal fins.

A newer strain of Platy Variatus is the Black Wagtail Tuxedo in which all the fins are black and the body almost completely colored black. ◀

The new Redtail Tuxedo Platy Variatus (female shown here), may have yellow or pink dorsal and anal fins. ◀

◗ This is a male Redtail Tuxedo Platy Variatus. Notice the modification of the anal fin when compared to the normal anal fin which females possess.

▶ Platy Variatus names are usually given by the first fish farm to market the variety. This fish has been known as the Milk and Ink Redtail Variatus as well as the Salt and Pepper Tuxedo Variatus. This fish is a male.

◀ The most spectacular of the Platy Variatus is the hifin Marigold with the bright golden yellow body and red fins.

◀ The black in this Black Variatus male occurs over a red body or a yellow body. Very frequently these highly pigmented fish develop melanoma cancer. This is a male.

▲ This female Redtail Tuxedo Platy Variatus has the basic golden color of most *variatus* found in the wild. The range of *variatus* is from the Rio Panuco to the Rio Cazones in eastern Mexico.

▲ This Marigold Platy Variatus does not have the red color in the dorsal as some strains.

▲ A normal male Marigold Variatus. This strain has a highly colored dorsal and tail fin.

▶ A female Blue Variatus, one of the earliest Platy Variatus types.

▶ Gold or Marigold Platy Variatus male. This strain has a red tail with black edging on the dorsal and tail. The dark scales on the side of the body are considered distractions.

▲ This is often called the Ghost Platy Variatus but may be marketed under many other names including Salt and Pepper Redtail Variatus.

▶ This is a Marigold Wagtail Variatus. The black markings in the fins are not as unique as those in the *maculatus* platies.

◀ The Red Marigold Platy Variatus males stay small in most cases.

▶ This is a female Platy Variatus that is a throwback to the wild strain and lacks any special colors.

▲ This is a Salt and Pepper Blue Platy Variatus with a phenomenal dorsal and tail fin coloration

CATFISHES

CATFISHES are called *catfishes* because they have whiskers. The catfishes presented here are all from South America because that's where most aquarium catfishes originate. I have also selected only those catfishes which stay on the bottom most of the time. There are a thousand catfishes found on every continent in the world but most of them are unsuitable for the aquarium because they are too large or swallow anything they can grab. Most have small, beady eyes yet they are nocturnal. All are egg layers. Some merely paste their eggs and leave them to hatch on their own, while others may sit on them like chickens. Aquarists utilize these catfishes as scavengers. The suckermouth catfishes eat the algae as quickly as it grows.

Platydoras costatus is a very beautiful catfish with strong spines along the sides. ▶

This unidentified *Hypostomus* is often called the Snowflake Hypostomus. ➡

This unidentified *Hypostomus* is called the Starry Night Hypostomus. ▼

This unidentified *Hypostomus* is called the Sunshine Gold Dragon. ➡

Many *Hypostomus* look like this one and have no scientific name.

Corydoras imitator. ▼

The Black and Tan *Hypostomus* has not yet been scientifically described. ➡

◀ Blotchy Plecostomus is really a *Hypostomus* species.

The Long-tail *Hypostomus*. ▼

This is called the Leopard *Hypostomus* because of its black spots. ▼

The Green *Hypostomus*.

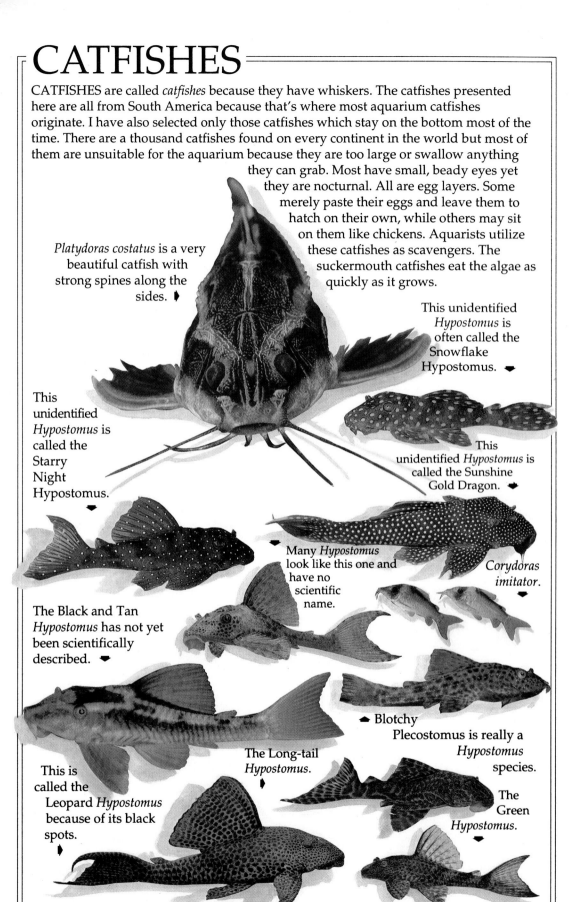

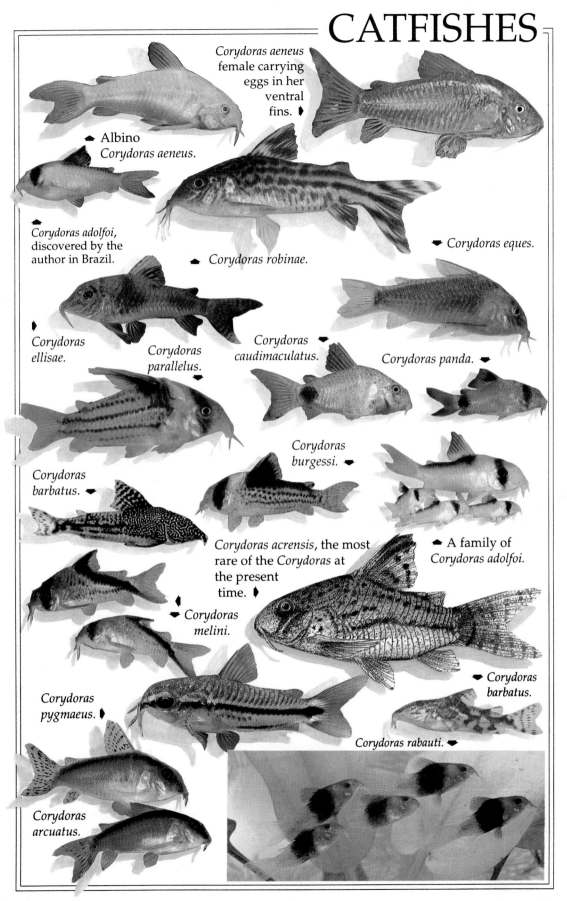

CATFISHES

Corydoras aeneus female carrying eggs in her ventral fins.

Albino *Corydoras aeneus.*

Corydoras adolfoi, discovered by the author in Brazil.

Corydoras robinae.

Corydoras eques.

Corydoras ellisae.

Corydoras parallelus.

Corydoras caudimaculatus.

Corydoras panda.

Corydoras burgessi.

Corydoras barbatus.

Corydoras acrensis, the most rare of the *Corydoras* at the present time.

A family of *Corydoras adolfoi.*

Corydoras melini.

Corydoras pygmaeus.

Corydoras barbatus.

Corydoras rabauti.

Corydoras arcuatus.

MALAWI CICHLIDS

MALAWI CICHLIDS are not fish for the beginner. They are very territorial and extremely combative. Coming from Lake Malawi in Malawi, Africa, the fishes live among stone reefs where they occupy small crevices or caves in which they breed and raise their families. They are almost exclusively maternal mouth brooders. The female stores the eggs and newly hatched fry in her mouth until they are old enough (about one month) to fend for themselves. There are several books written just about Malawi cichlids.

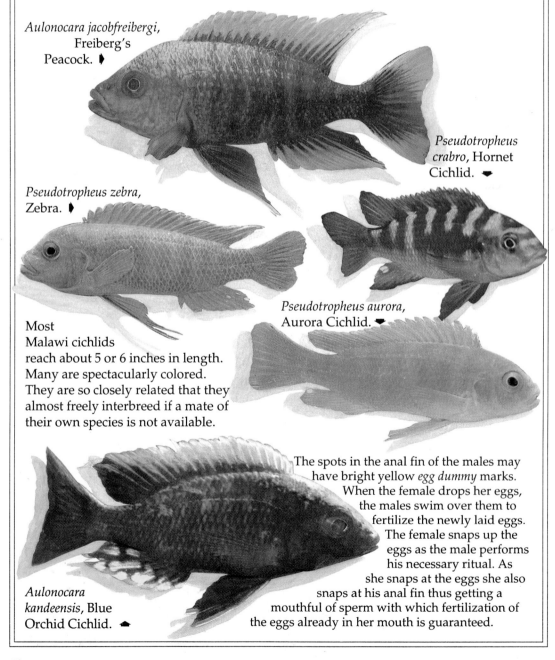

Aulonocara jacobfreibergi, Freiberg's Peacock. ▶

Pseudotropheus crabro, Hornet Cichlid. ◄

Pseudotropheus zebra, Zebra. ▶

Pseudotropheus aurora, Aurora Cichlid. ◄

Most Malawi cichlids reach about 5 or 6 inches in length. Many are spectacularly colored. They are so closely related that they almost freely interbreed if a mate of their own species is not available.

The spots in the anal fin of the males may have bright yellow *egg dummy* marks. When the female drops her eggs, the males swim over them to fertilize the newly laid eggs. The female snaps up the eggs as the male performs his necessary ritual. As she snaps at the eggs she also snaps at his anal fin thus getting a mouthful of sperm with which fertilization of the eggs already in her mouth is guaranteed.

Aulonocara kandeensis, Blue Orchid Cichlid. ◄

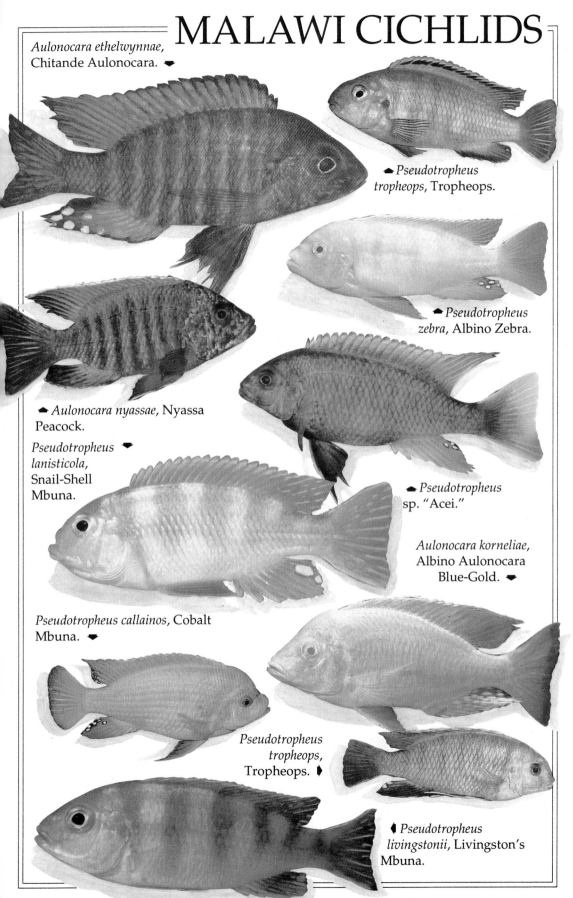

MALAWI CICHLIDS

Aulonocara ethelwynnae, Chitande Aulonocara. ➤

Pseudotropheus tropheops, Tropheops.

Pseudotropheus zebra, Albino Zebra.

➤ *Aulonocara nyassae,* Nyassa Peacock.

Pseudotropheus lanisticola, Snail-Shell Mbuna.

➤ *Pseudotropheus* sp. "Acei."

Aulonocara korneliae, Albino Aulonocara Blue-Gold. ➤

Pseudotropheus callainos, Cobalt Mbuna. ➤

Pseudotropheus tropheops, Tropheops. ➤

◀ *Pseudotropheus livingstonii,* Livingston's Mbuna.

ANGELFISH

ANGELFISHES are found in the freshwater lakes and rivers of South America. There are fishes found in the ocean which are also called *angelfishes*, but these are not related to the freshwater angelfishes. They earned the name *angelfishes* because they seem to float around the aquarium like an angel; they are also very peaceful to any fish which is too large to be swallowed whole. While they can exist on dried foods, they do prefer some living foods like live brine shrimp, *Daphnia* and tubifex worms. These foods are available at most pet shops.

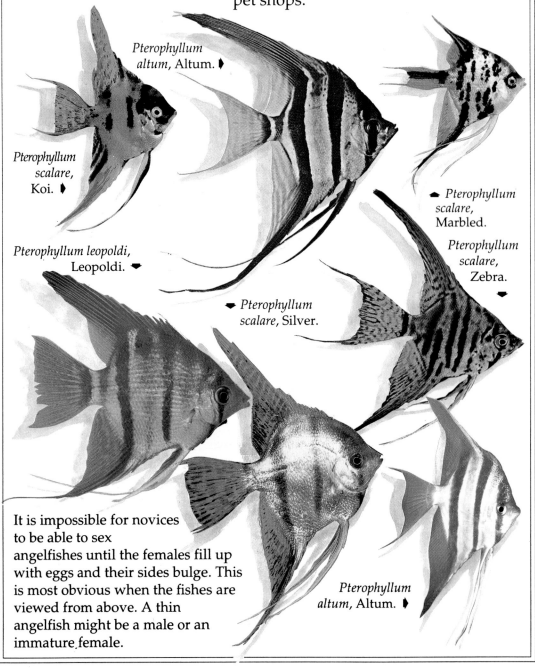

Pterophyllum altum, Altum. ▶

Pterophyllum scalare, Koi. ▶

Pterophyllum scalare, Marbled. ◀

Pterophyllum leopoldi, Leopoldi. ◀

Pterophyllum scalare, Zebra. ▼

Pterophyllum scalare, Silver. ◀

Pterophyllum altum, Altum. ▶

It is impossible for novices to be able to sex angelfishes until the females fill up with eggs and their sides bulge. This is most obvious when the fishes are viewed from above. A thin angelfish might be a male or an immature female.

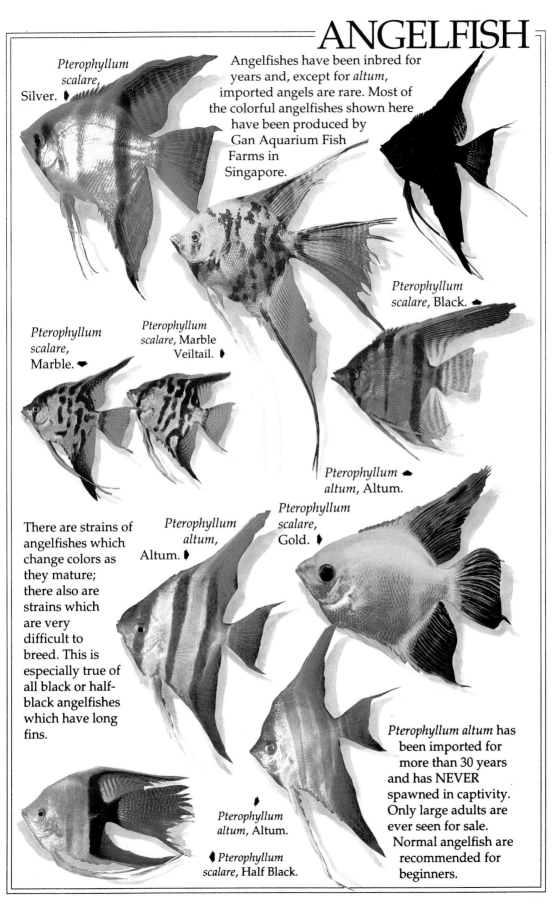

ANGELFISH

Pterophyllum scalare, Silver. ▶

Angelfishes have been inbred for years and, except for *altum*, imported angels are rare. Most of the colorful angelfishes shown here have been produced by Gan Aquarium Fish Farms in Singapore.

Pterophyllum scalare, Black. ◀

Pterophyllum scalare, Marble. ◀

Pterophyllum scalare, Marble Veiltail. ▶

Pterophyllum altum, Altum. ◀

There are strains of angelfishes which change colors as they mature; there also are strains which are very difficult to breed. This is especially true of all black or half-black angelfishes which have long fins.

Pterophyllum altum, Altum. ▶

Pterophyllum scalare, Gold. ▶

Pterophyllum altum, Altum. ▲

◀ *Pterophyllum scalare,* Half Black.

Pterophyllum altum has been imported for more than 30 years and has NEVER spawned in captivity. Only large adults are ever seen for sale. Normal angelfish are recommended for beginners.

DANIOS

Danios are delightful and trouble-free in the aquarium. They are peaceful schooling fishes that should have a long, shallow tank. In fact, they will spawn in water that is only 4 to 6 inches deep. The water temperature should be in the mid to upper 70s F. The water should be clean and well-aerated, but the pH and hardness are not important as long as extremes are avoided. One caution: Danios are jumpers. The tank must be well covered!

Danio malabaricus, Giant Danio. ↓

Danios are cyprinids, as are Goldfish, Koi, Barbs, and Minnows. Some cyprinids are coldwater fishes, but Danios are among the tropical members of this same large family. Danios are brightly colored, active fishes that have long barbels. There are many species, mostly from India and Malaysia and surrounding areas.

Brachydanio nigrofasciatus, Spotted Danio. ↓ ↑

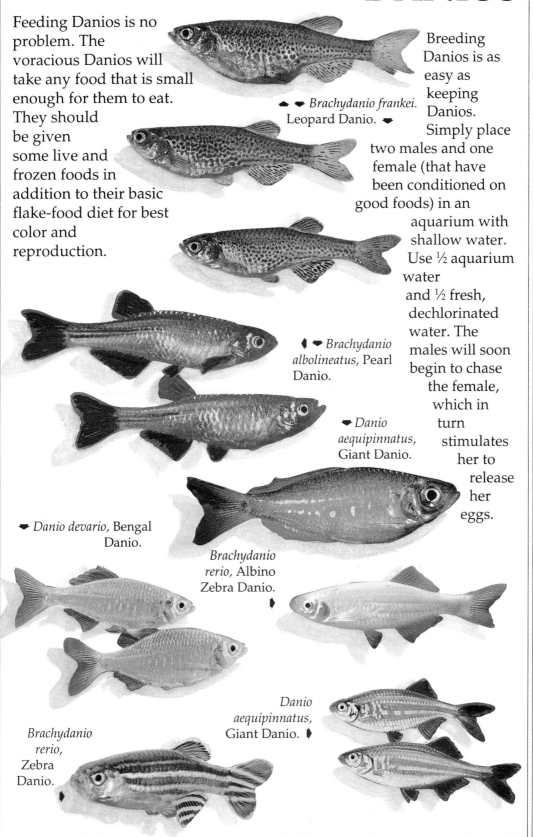

Feeding Danios is no problem. The voracious Danios will take any food that is small enough for them to eat. They should be given some live and frozen foods in addition to their basic flake-food diet for best color and reproduction.

Breeding Danios is as easy as keeping Danios. Simply place two males and one female (that have been conditioned on good foods) in an aquarium with shallow water. Use ½ aquarium water and ½ fresh, dechlorinated water. The males will soon begin to chase the female, which in turn stimulates her to release her eggs.

Brachydanio frankei. Leopard Danio.

Brachydanio albolineatus, Pearl Danio.

Danio aequipinnatus, Giant Danio.

Danio devario, Bengal Danio.

Brachydanio rerio, Albino Zebra Danio.

Brachydanio rerio, Zebra Danio.

Danio aequipinnatus, Giant Danio.

RASBORA

Rasboras are handsome, active fish that are natives of the Far East. They like to swim in small schools and are shy when kept alone. A school of Rasboras in a planted tank that receives a little sunlight will convince anyone of their true beauty.

Feeding Rasboras is definitely not a problem. As long as the food—live, frozen, or flake—is small enough for their tiny mouths, they will eat it with relish.

Be careful about overfeeding. Even though they take the food with gusto, they are small fishes and quickly eat their fill.

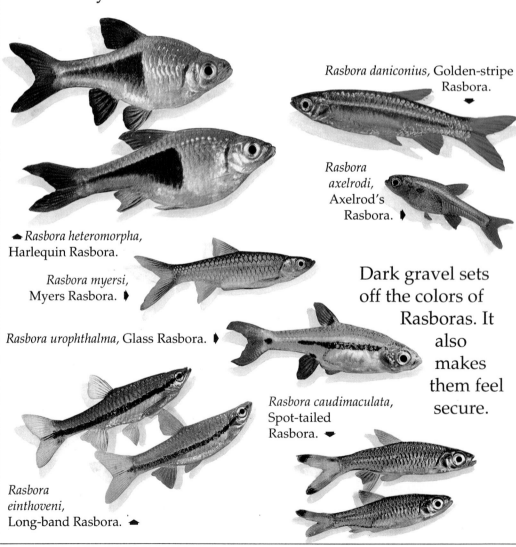

Rasbora dorsiocellata, Hi-spot Rasbora.

Rasbora daniconius, Golden-stripe Rasbora.

Rasbora axelrodi, Axelrod's Rasbora.

Rasbora heteromorpha, Harlequin Rasbora.

Rasbora myersi, Myers Rasbora.

Rasbora urophthalma, Glass Rasbora.

Dark gravel sets off the colors of Rasboras. It also makes them feel secure.

Rasbora caudimaculata, Spot-tailed Rasbora.

Rasbora einthoveni, Long-band Rasbora.

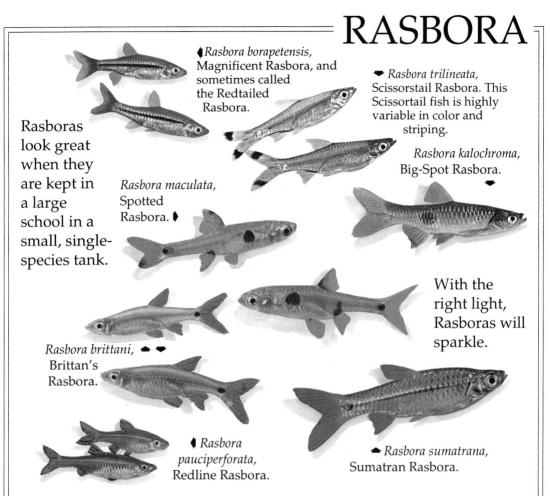

◀*Rasbora borapetensis,* Magnificent Rasbora, and sometimes called the Redtailed Rasbora.

➤ *Rasbora trilineata,* Scissorstail Rasbora. This Scissortail fish is highly variable in color and striping.

Rasbora kalochroma, Big-Spot Rasbora. ➤

Rasboras look great when they are kept in a large school in a small, single-species tank.

Rasbora maculata, Spotted Rasbora. ▶

With the right light, Rasboras will sparkle.

Rasbora brittani, ◆ ➤ Brittan's Rasbora.

◀ *Rasbora pauciperforata,* Redline Rasbora.

◆*Rasbora sumatrana,* Sumatran Rasbora.

◆*Rasbora trilineata,* Scissorstail Rasbora.

Rasbora heteromorpha espei, Espei's Rasbora, spawning on a leaf. ➤

A Rasbora is a fast-swimming, exuberant fish that will leap to its death through the smallest opening in the tank cover. Keep this in mind and provide a secure cover and a long tank.

Most Rasboras are egg-scatterers. When the female fills with roe, the male chases her through the plants where she releases her tiny eggs. Unless the parents are removed from the tank, they will quickly eat the eggs. This is why there are so few egglayer fry found in the community tank. There are pairs spawning constantly in most communities, but the parents and other fishes eat the eggs as soon as they are laid.

MOLLIES

The name MOLLIES derives from the genus *Mollienesia* which is apparently misspelled because it was named to honor a French clergyman named Mollen. In 1963 the genus *Mollienesia* was merged into *Poecilia*, a move with which I do not agree because Mollies are very different from Guppies! In any case, these fishes are basically brackish or marine species and only thrive in hard, alkaline water. For this reason they are raised in huge quantities in the hard, alkaline water near the Gulf of Mexico in Florida. They are best kept alone since they do best in slightly brackish water with lots of soft vegetable matter in their diets.

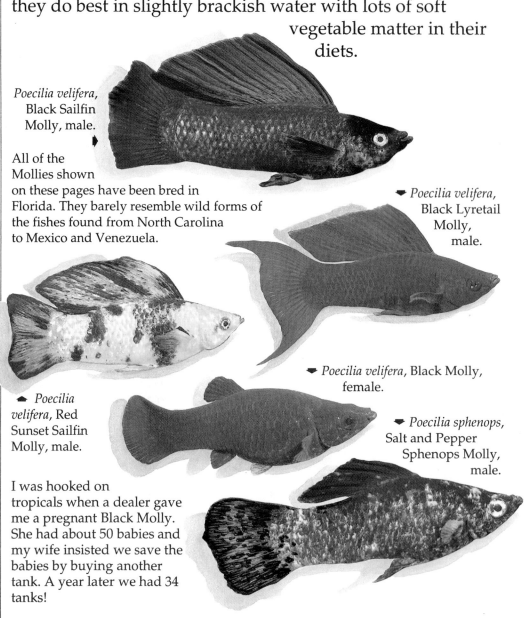

Poecilia velifera, Black Sailfin Molly, male.

All of the Mollies shown on these pages have been bred in Florida. They barely resemble wild forms of the fishes found from North Carolina to Mexico and Venezuela.

Poecilia velifera, Black Lyretail Molly, male.

Poecilia velifera, Red Sunset Sailfin Molly, male.

Poecilia velifera, Black Molly, female.

Poecilia sphenops, Salt and Pepper Sphenops Molly, male.

I was hooked on tropicals when a dealer gave me a pregnant Black Molly. She had about 50 babies and my wife insisted we save the babies by buying another tank. A year later we had 34 tanks!

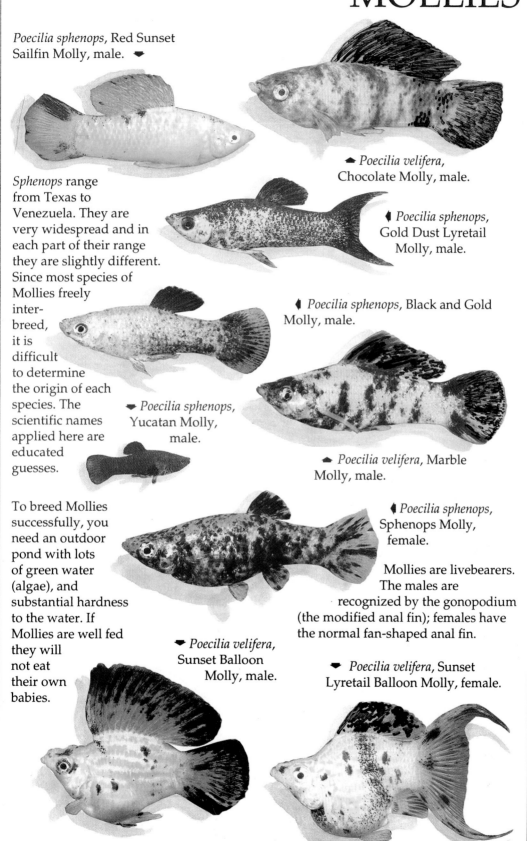

Poecilia sphenops, Red Sunset Sailfin Molly, male. ➥

Sphenops range from Texas to Venezuela. They are very widespread and in each part of their range they are slightly different. Since most species of Mollies freely inter-breed, it is difficult to determine the origin of each species. The scientific names applied here are educated guesses.

➥ *Poecilia velifera*, Chocolate Molly, male.

◀ *Poecilia sphenops*, Gold Dust Lyretail Molly, male.

◀ *Poecilia sphenops*, Black and Gold Molly, male.

➥ *Poecilia sphenops*, Yucatan Molly, male.

➥ *Poecilia velifera*, Marble Molly, male.

To breed Mollies successfully, you need an outdoor pond with lots of green water (algae), and substantial hardness to the water. If Mollies are well fed they will not eat their own babies.

◀ *Poecilia sphenops*, Sphenops Molly, female.

Mollies are livebearers. The males are recognized by the gonopodium (the modified anal fin); females have the normal fan-shaped anal fin.

➥ *Poecilia velifera*, Sunset Balloon Molly, male.

➥ *Poecilia velifera*, Sunset Lyretail Balloon Molly, female.

MOLLIES

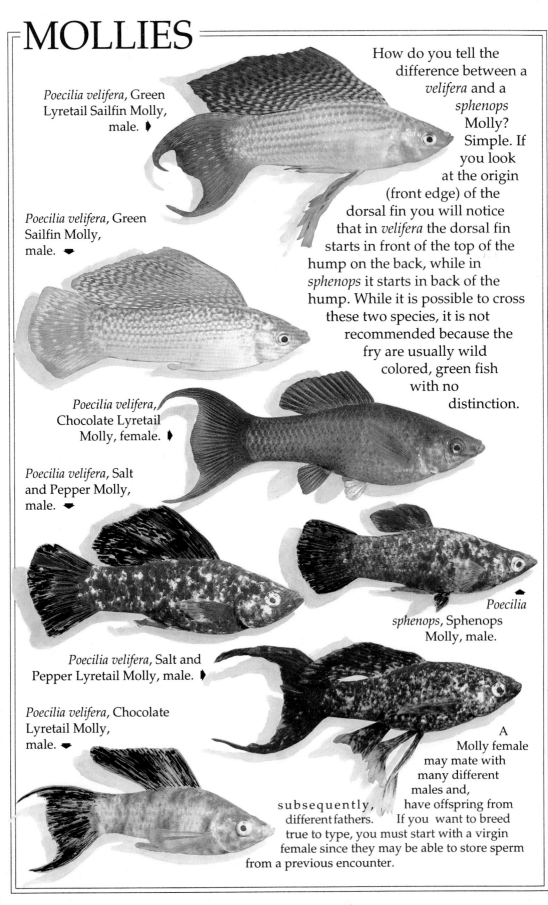

Poecilia velifera, Green Lyretail Sailfin Molly, male. ▶

Poecilia velifera, Green Sailfin Molly, male. ◀

Poecilia velifera, Chocolate Lyretail Molly, female. ▶

Poecilia velifera, Salt and Pepper Molly, male. ◀

Poecilia velifera, Salt and Pepper Lyretail Molly, male. ▶

Poecilia velifera, Chocolate Lyretail Molly, male. ◀

Poecilia sphenops, Sphenops Molly, male.

How do you tell the difference between a *velifera* and a *sphenops* Molly? Simple. If you look at the origin (front edge) of the dorsal fin you will notice that in *velifera* the dorsal fin starts in front of the top of the hump on the back, while in *sphenops* it starts in back of the hump. While it is possible to cross these two species, it is not recommended because the fry are usually wild colored, green fish with no distinction.

A Molly female may mate with many different males and, subsequently, have offspring from different fathers. If you want to breed true to type, you must start with a virgin female since they may be able to store sperm from a previous encounter.

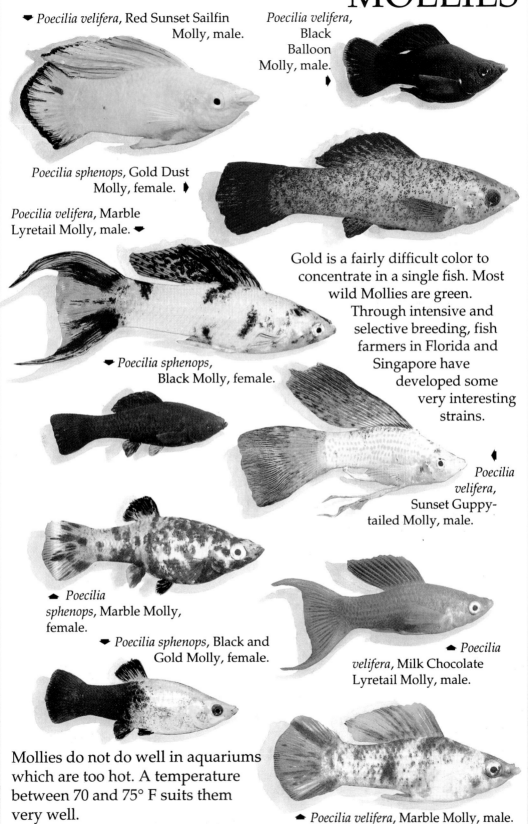

Poecilia velifera, Red Sunset Sailfin Molly, male.

Poecilia velifera, Black Balloon Molly, male.

Poecilia sphenops, Gold Dust Molly, female.

Poecilia velifera, Marble Lyretail Molly, male.

Gold is a fairly difficult color to concentrate in a single fish. Most wild Mollies are green. Through intensive and selective breeding, fish farmers in Florida and Singapore have developed some very interesting strains.

Poecilia sphenops, Black Molly, female.

Poecilia velifera, Sunset Guppy-tailed Molly, male.

Poecilia sphenops, Marble Molly, female.

Poecilia sphenops, Black and Gold Molly, female.

Poecilia velifera, Milk Chocolate Lyretail Molly, male.

Mollies do not do well in aquariums which are too hot. A temperature between 70 and 75° F suits them very well.

Poecilia velifera, Marble Molly, male.

51

PLATIES

The name PLATIES originates from the now obsolete genus name *Platypoecilus*, the original genus in which these fishes were found. These interesting livebearers have become an aquarium favorite and one of the major fishes produced in the large fish farms in Florida. Dozens of varieties are produced, many with swordtail 'blood' in them as swordtails and platies easily hybridize. As with all livebearers, the males have a modified anal fin called a *gonopodium* with which they impregnate the females. Sexual contacts between males and females is an often repeated ritual. Females produce about 30-75 fry every month.

◀ Gold Wagtail Platy.

◄ This magnificent Platy is called a *Salt-and-Pepper Red Wagtail Platy Variatus*. Its bloodlines are a mystery.

▶ Red Wagtail Highfin Platy.

▶ Gold Meteor Moon Platy.

▶ Very rare albino Wagtail Platies. Obviously the black in the fins is suppressed.

Marigold Meteor Platies. ◄

These Black Wagtail Platies are derived from 2 strains. The solid black (below) is sometimes called a *Black Moon Red Wagtail* while the other (left) is a *Red Wagtail.* ◀ ◄

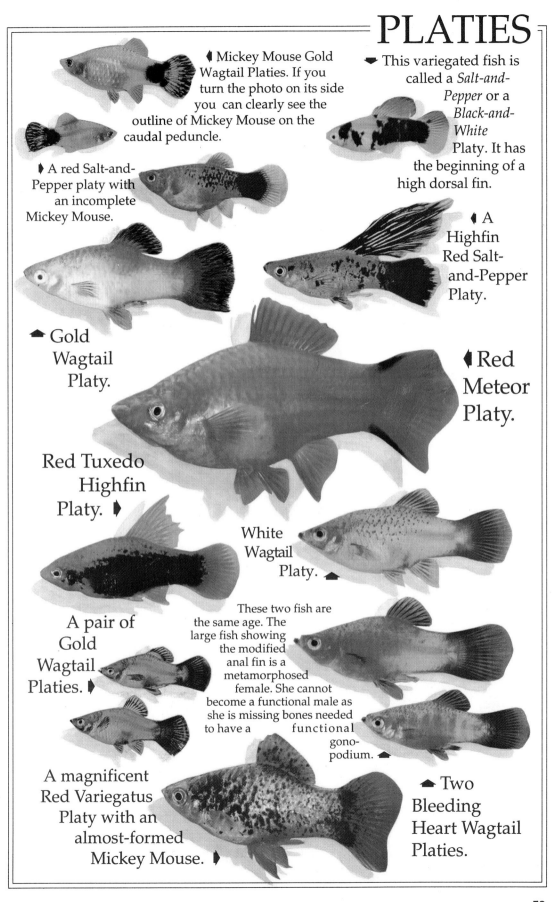

◀ Mickey Mouse Gold Wagtail Platies. If you turn the photo on its side you can clearly see the outline of Mickey Mouse on the caudal peduncle.

↖ This variegated fish is called a *Salt-and-Pepper* or a *Black-and-White* Platy. It has the beginning of a high dorsal fin.

◀ A red Salt-and-Pepper platy with an incomplete Mickey Mouse.

◀ A Highfin Red Salt-and-Pepper Platy.

↖ Gold Wagtail Platy.

◀ Red Meteor Platy.

Red Tuxedo Highfin Platy. ▶

White Wagtail Platy. ▲

A pair of Gold Wagtail Platies. ▶

These two fish are the same age. The large fish showing the modified anal fin is a metamorphosed female. She cannot become a functional male as she is missing bones needed to have a functional gonopodium. ◀

A magnificent Red Variegatus Platy with an almost-formed Mickey Mouse. ▶

▲ Two Bleeding Heart Wagtail Platies.

GUPPIES

The name GUPPY originated in an obsolete scientific name which honored the discoverer, a Mr.Lechmere Guppy. The scientific and common name of this has changed several times, but everybody understands the word *guppy*. This is a livebearer which has broods every month. Males and females are different with the males possessing most of the color and finnage variations. True-breeding strains are very rare and while these fish are easy to breed, they are very difficult to raise to their maximum size with all males identical. These are probably the easiest aquarium fish to keep and breed.

Wild male guppy from Trinidad.

Wild male guppy from Guyana.

Black flame veiltail guppy.

Red veiltail guppy.

Black veiltail guppy.

Red flagtail guppy.

Poor quality double swordtail guppy.

Gold pintail guppies.

Gold bottom swordtail guppy.

Bottom swordtail snakeskin guppy.

Lower swordtail black guppy with banner dorsal.

Red lower swordtail guppy.

Blonde lower swordtail guppy.

Wild-colored lower swordtail guppy.

GUPPIES

Blue veiltail guppy.

Black fantail guppies. Two males and a female.

Blue fantail with white dorsal.

Snakeskin guppy with upper swordtail and long dorsal.

Flame lower swordtail guppy.

Black fantail guppy.

Gold fantail guppy.

Double swordtail white guppy.

Leopard fantail guppy.

Red flame veiltail guppy.

Gold throwback guppy.

Black white-tail guppy.

Gold flame fantail guppy.

Two strains of double swordtail guppies.

Poor quality gold guppy.

Gold snakeskin veiltail guppy.

DISCUS

The name DISCUS originates from the scientific name *Symphysodon discus* Heckel. Since the original description about 150 years ago, additional species and subspecies have been discovered (several by the author of this book!) The fishes shown here were produced at the Gan Aquarium Fish Farm in Singapore. There are many similar Discus and each breeder has his own name for the particular variety. These are peaceful fish but best kept in their own tank accompanied only by peaceful Catfish and Cardinal Tetras.

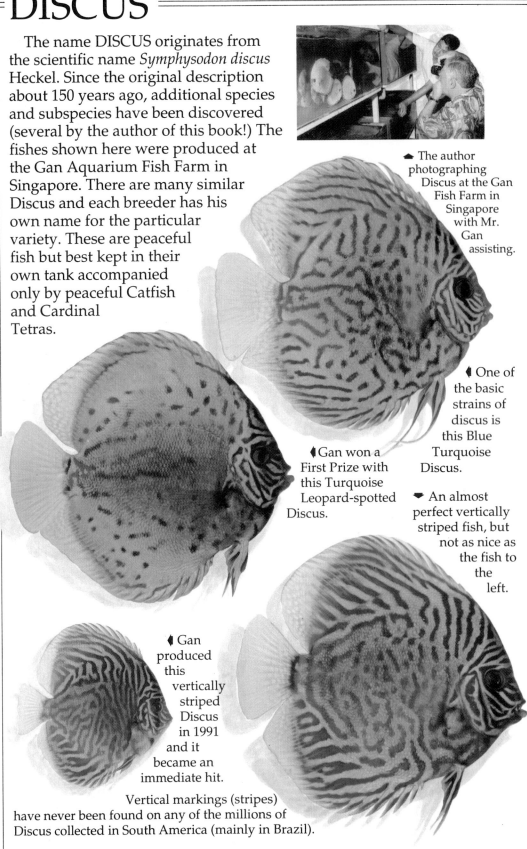

◆ The author photographing Discus at the Gan Fish Farm in Singapore with Mr. Gan assisting.

◆ One of the basic strains of discus is this Blue Turquoise Discus.

◆Gan won a First Prize with this Turquoise Leopard-spotted Discus.

◆ An almost perfect vertically striped fish, but not as nice as the fish to the left.

◆ Gan produced this vertically striped Discus in 1991 and it became an immediate hit.

Vertical markings (stripes) have never been found on any of the millions of Discus collected in South America (mainly in Brazil).

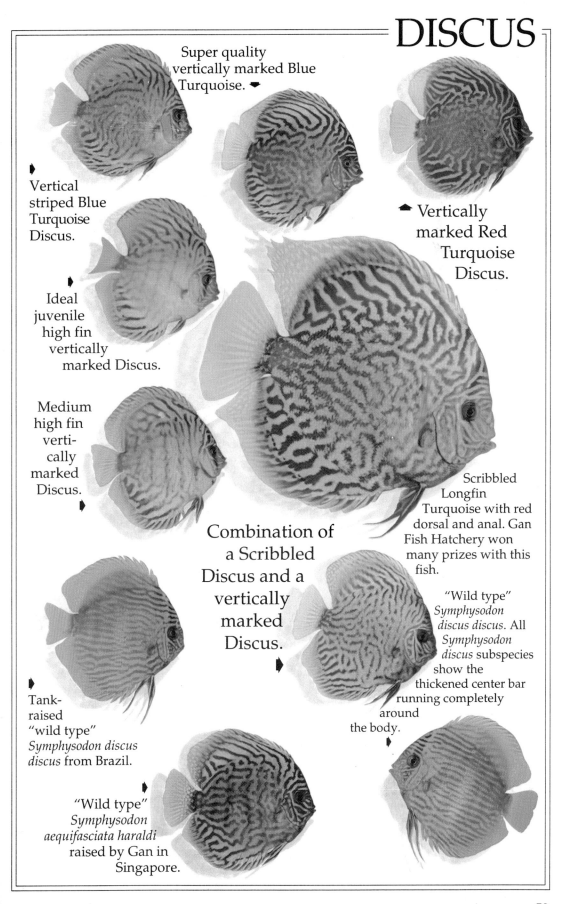

DISCUS

Super quality vertically marked Blue Turquoise.

Vertical striped Blue Turquoise Discus.

Ideal juvenile high fin vertically marked Discus.

◄ Vertically marked Red Turquoise Discus.

Medium high fin vertically marked Discus.

Combination of a Scribbled Discus and a vertically marked Discus.

Scribbled Longfin Turquoise with red dorsal and anal. Gan Fish Hatchery won many prizes with this fish.

Tankraised "wild type" *Symphysodon discus discus* from Brazil.

"Wild type" *Symphysodon discus discus*. All *Symphysodon discus* subspecies show the thickened center bar running completely around the body.

"Wild type" *Symphysodon aequifasciata haraldi* raised by Gan in Singapore.

DISCUS

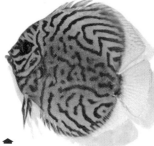

The vertical stripes on this Turquoise Discus are remarkable. ▶

Fewer, but wider, vertical stripes made this Blue Turquoise a champion for Gan Aquarium Fish Farm in Singapore.

◀ A poorly marked Red Turquoise which has wide stripes but they are horizontal, not vertical.

Stripes or no stripes...this Blue Discus has no stripes at all. ▶

This is the latest 1993 model of Discus markings, a yellow discus with a few or no blue stripes and speckled with irregular black blotches.

▲ A magnificently colored Blue Turquoise Scribbled Discus. Bright red eyes are an asset for Discus.

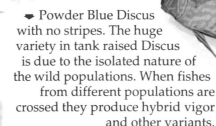

◀ Powder Blue Discus with no stripes. The huge variety in tank raised Discus is due to the isolated nature of the wild populations. When fishes from different populations are crossed they produce hybrid vigor and other variants.

◀ The Blue Discus with no stripes now has long fins.

▶ The Powder Blue Discus with no body markings.

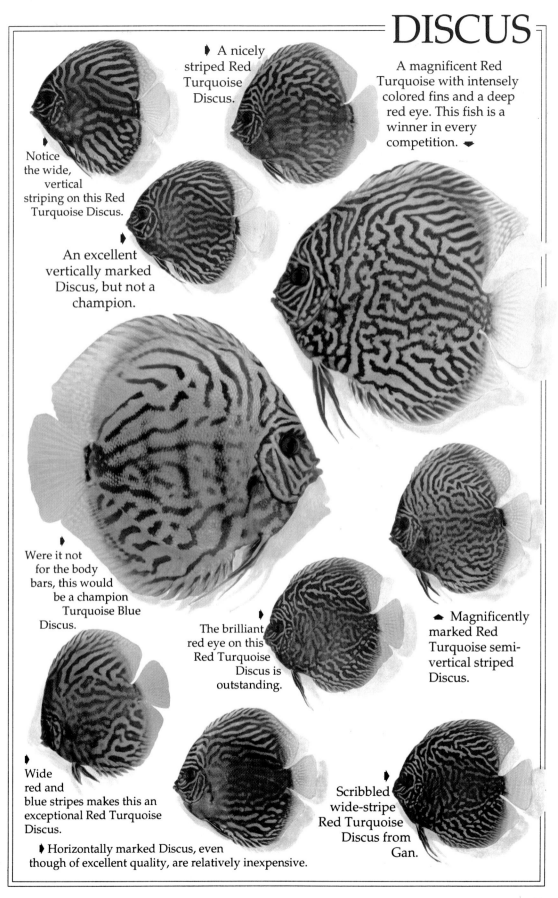

DISCUS

A nicely striped Red Turquoise Discus.

A magnificent Red Turquoise with intensely colored fins and a deep red eye. This fish is a winner in every competition.

Notice the wide, vertical striping on this Red Turquoise Discus.

An excellent vertically marked Discus, but not a champion.

Were it not for the body bars, this would be a champion Turquoise Blue Discus.

The brilliant red eye on this Red Turquoise Discus is outstanding.

Magnificently marked Red Turquoise semi-vertical striped Discus.

Wide red and blue stripes makes this an exceptional Red Turquoise Discus.

Scribbled wide-stripe Red Turquoise Discus from Gan.

Horizontally marked Discus, even though of excellent quality, are relatively inexpensive.

GOURAMIS

Gouramis, Bettas, and Paradise Fish are all labyrinthfishes, which means they can breathe air when their waters become too poor in oxygen. Most labyrinthfishes are bubblenest builders. The male blows bubbles on the surface of the water and the eggs are placed into (or float into) the bubblenest after they are released by the female.

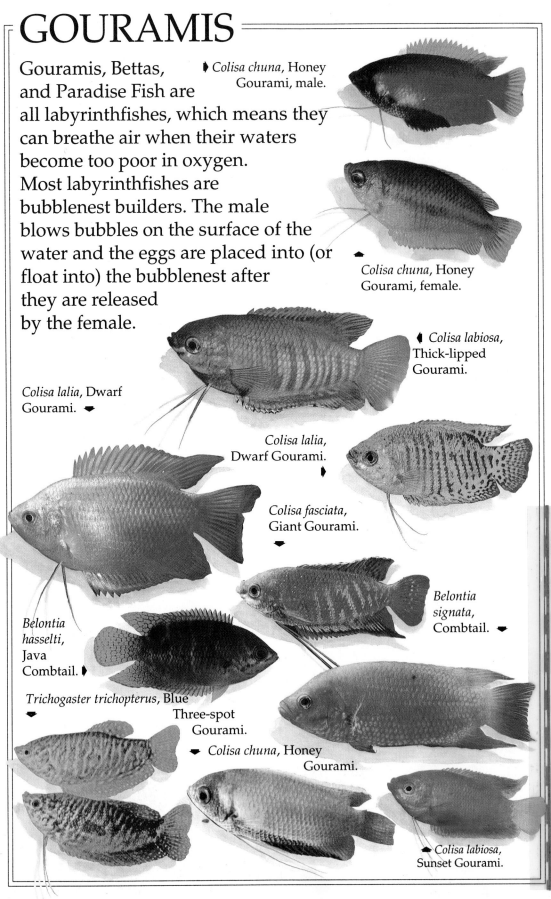

◀ *Colisa chuna*, Honey Gourami, male.

Colisa chuna, Honey Gourami, female.

◀ *Colisa labiosa*, Thick-lipped Gourami.

Colisa lalia, Dwarf Gourami. ➡

Colisa lalia, Dwarf Gourami.

Colisa fasciata, Giant Gourami.

Belontia signata, Combtail. ➡

Belontia hasselti, Java Combtail. ➡

Trichogaster trichopterus, Blue Three-spot Gourami.

➡ *Colisa chuna*, Honey Gourami.

➡ *Colisa labiosa*, Sunset Gourami.

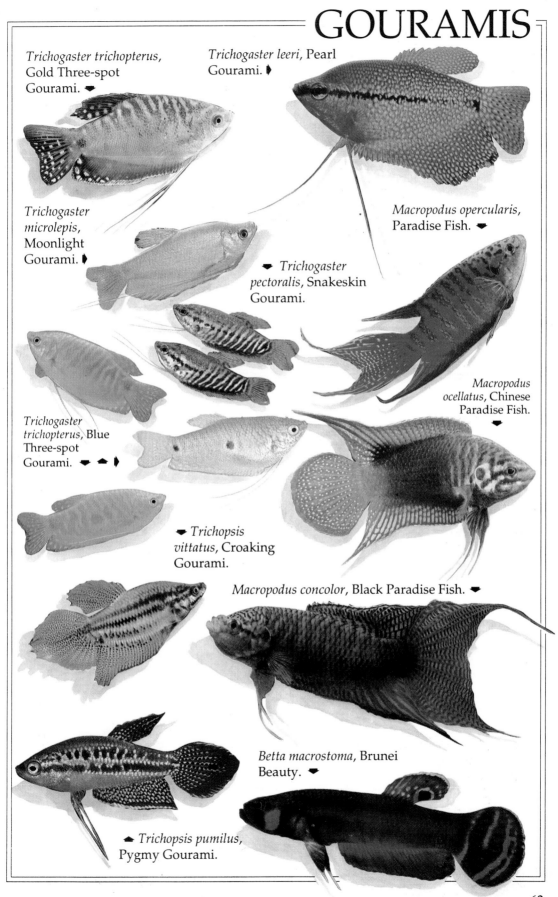

Trichogaster trichopterus, Gold Three-spot Gourami. ◄

Trichogaster leeri, Pearl Gourami. ▶

Trichogaster microlepis, Moonlight Gourami. ▶

◄ *Trichogaster pectoralis,* Snakeskin Gourami.

Macropodus opercularis, Paradise Fish. ◄

Macropodus ocellatus, Chinese Paradise Fish. ▼

Trichogaster trichopterus, Blue Three-spot Gourami. ◄ ◄ ▶

◄ *Trichopsis vittatus,* Croaking Gourami.

Macropodus concolor, Black Paradise Fish. ◄

Betta macrostoma, Brunei Beauty. ◄

◄ *Trichopsis pumilus,* Pygmy Gourami.

OTHER BOOKS BY T.F.H.

PS-703, 384 pages
Over 450 color photos

PS-601, 128 pages
70 color photos

F-10, 32 pages

PS-834, 200 pages

CO-013S, 128 pages
147 color photos

YF-100, 32 pages

TS-139, 144 pages
Over 240 color photos

H-946, 320 pages
188 color photos

H-963, 320 pages
161 color photos

H-966, 448 pages
244 color photos

CO-002S, 128 pages
88 color photos

CO-003S, 128 pages
83 color photos

SK-033, 64 pages
Over 50 color photos

TU-016, 64 pages
93 color photos

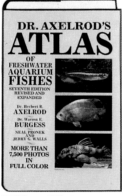

H-1077, over 1150 pages
Over 7000 color photos

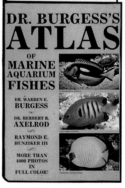

H-1100, 736 pages
Over 4000 color photos

TS-104, 192 pages

These and thousands of other animal books have been published by T.F.H. T.F.H. is the world's largest publisher of animal books. You can find our titles at the same place you bought this one, or write to us for a free catalog.